Bedrooms and Bathrooms

Haynes
THE BOOK ®

Contents

Very easy

A little skill

Some experience

Before you Begin

Bedrooms and bathrooms are the only two rooms in the house where you don't need to accommodate the likes and dislikes of others or the endless practicalities which can govern the choice of colour, fabric or room style. The only really practical considerations are that the hard core bedding – the sheets, pillow covers and duvets are easy to wash and launder and that the fabrics chosen are the very best you can afford.

The projects in this book use only basic methods and stitches, adaptable to any situation and assembled by hand or machine. The fabrics have been chosen for their timeless appeal and availability.

This chapter introduces the basic ingredients needed to complete the projects – fabrics, lining, trimmings – giving hints on colour and style and guidance on finding the right combination of materials and equipment to complete the project.

Style and colour

Almost any fabric or style of furnishing can be used to decorate a bedroom – whether your preference is for an intimate feminine room or for something in rustic country style. Whether you have a tiny box room or a huge mansion room, the choice and execution of ideas are infinite.

GRAND OR COUNTRY STYLE

▲▼ The finest cotton organdie, silk organza, muslin and embroidered lawn can be used in swathes and massed fullness to create the most romantic of bedrooms. For the country look, use woollen tweeds, rough handloomed linens, and patchwork covers to complement rustic furnishings. The combinations are endless.

PURE WHITE

▲ Whites and creams are very light and ethereal but can be just too naive unless set off with touches of colour. A terracotta floor, colour stained wood, cushions or a lampshade bring a good balance of colour to an all white room, helping to frame the delicate appearance of the fabric.

FRENCH STYLE

▲ Toile de jouy is a traditional French printed cotton which is perfect for bedrooms. Much copied in essence, if not in quality, it is available at every price level. It has the great advantage of being a pattern without confusing or strong colour combinations, the soft cotton falls and drapes well, is usually washable and always good to handle.

COLOUR COMBINATIONS

▲ There really are no hard and fast rules to follow but bright colours such as sharp yellow, turquoise and lime greens aren't great for the complexion first thing in the morning, and colours should generally be soft in tone. If you want to use rich colours – reds/greens/dark blues, always try to choose those with softer under tones – i.e. a mulberry tone red rather than a purply tone.

SMALL DETAIL

◀ Pay attention to the small accessories - always have a vase of flowers however small, for colour and perfume. Good lighting, a mirror and a chair to sit on; somewhere to drop your clothes and somewhere to comb your hair are as important as the fabric and soft furnishings.

CREAMY TONES

▲ Chic, elegant rooms depend on the subtle combinations of taupes, oysters, sands, and creamy tones. Textures are vital to bring the scheme to life and here great use can be made of knitted fabrics, leather, suede, cashmere, velvets, brushed cottons and silks.

Choosing fabrics

High quality bedding really does help towards getting a good nights sleep. However luxurious your bed and flamboyant the drapes – the sheets, blankets and duvets must be of the best quality that you can afford. Where possible use linen, a linen and cotton mix or a good quality soft cotton, they absorb moisture and will stay soft over many years of use and laundering.

LINEN

▲ From the earliest times the finest linen sheets have been prized possessions and important enough to be noted in the inventories of the grandest houses. Linen fibre is obtained from the flax plant, grown mostly in northern Europe. Time consuming to produce and therefore relatively expensive, linen has no equal when it comes to bedding. Soft, strong and very absorbent, linen can be washed at high temperatures and will take years to wear out.

COTTON

▲ Cotton is second only to linen for bedding – available in every type of weave imaginable: waffle, twill, brushed, combed, satin, knitted, printed with floral or abstract designs, woven into stripes and checks. Cotton, like linen is robust, absorbs moisture and will stand up to a lifetime of washing at very high temperatures. Less expensive than linen, look for a fifty/fifty cotton linen mix which performs well and may better fit your budget.

PRINTS AND WEAVES

▲ Printed bedding in a multitude of colours can soon become tiresome: however, fine stripes and checks in pastel colours – blue, green, pink and yellow are fairly easy to find – and will ring the changes. They work well with both floral and plain white and can be added to spice up a tired scheme. Textured fabric is best avoided for sheeting as the rough surface may be uncomfortable to lie on but will make attractive cushions.

BUYING WIDE WIDTH FABRIC

▲ The normal width for furnishing fabric is 130cm – 150cm (50in – 60in). As almost all bedding is wider than this, it is helpful to buy fabric in a wider width. There are specialist mail order companies who supply fabric in 180cm – 325cm (72in – 130in) widths, this will save you joining seams. For a comforter/duvet/bedcover use this fabric on top, with a ready made sheet below.

POLYESTER/COTTON

◄ The plus points for polyester/cotton fabric are low cost and easy-care. Poly/cotton sheeting doesn't last anything like as long as pure cotton or linen, colours will fade with laundering and there just isn't the moisture absorbency that is so important for a comfortable nights sleep. If you are going to the effort of making your own bedding, buy the best fabric you can afford.

Using patterned fabric

One of the best reasons to decorate your bedroom is the opportunity to indulge in lovely fabrics – nowhere else in the house can you really please yourself, and nowhere else can you mix such a variety of different patterns and textures together.

PATTERN REPEATS

◄ Florals in the bedroom look very pretty and can introduce an important feminine touch, but a little of any pattern goes a long way. An infinite number of printed fabrics are available, ranging from a huge stylised design, to the tiniest dimity print. If you are using a fabric with either a printed or woven design you will need to take into account the repeat of the pattern. Choose a prominent part of the design – say the top of a large leaf or the bottom of a basket – and measure to the exact same spot on the next pattern up. This is your repeat. For each length (cut) of fabric you will need to check how your repeat will fit, and cut up to the next repeat. So, if a given length is 210cm (84in) and your pattern repeat is 65cm (26in), your cuts will include three and a bit complete patterns – i.e. 195cm (72in) for three repeats. Four repeats will bring the length to be cut to 260cm (104in). The 'off cuts' can be used for pillow frill or as trimmings.

THE CONTRASTS

▲ In one bed you could use linen sheets with printed cotton pillow covers; a cotton duvet patterned underneath and plaid on top; a throw made from the softest cashmere embroidered in subtle tones of oyster and taupe; silk drapes lined with cotton muslin. Extremely luxurious and expensive fabrics happily mixing with the inexpensive and ordinary. Or use the most ordinary fabric to create a romantic bed – imagine skirts in everyday black and white mattress ticking; dressed with crisp white sheets and pillows; draped all around with sprigged cotton lined with muslin and a pair of silk cushions in strong colours to provide the spark.

USING WHITES

◄ Patterned or strongly coloured sheets and pillows can be fun on occasion, but nothing beats the pure, unadulterated simplicity of white. Pure white or oyster; unbleached linen or parchment; whites are at ease with rich red, green or the softest, palest yellow or pink. Smart and unassuming, crisp and fresh in summer; providing a foil for heavy winter bedding, if you can only afford one set of sheets, make them white.

THE SEASONS

◄ Think of summer and winter covers and plan to make two sets of curtains, reversible comforters and bedcovers. Tartan and toile de jouy are perfect companions; the one crisp and fresh for summer, the other warm and comforting in winter. Primitive sprigged cottons with shot taffetas; country checks with rural tweeds or sensible wool curtains lined with floaty muslin organdie.

PREPARATION

Before you make any cuts, check the fabric thoroughly for flaws. Faults in the weave do happen in weaving and printing and the design size can vary a few centimetres from roll to roll. Carefully work out the pattern repeat, accommodating any small flaws in hems and headings. Cut along the grain for a plain fabric and to a pattern line for a print. Technically the pattern should be printed exactly on the grain but in reality this will only happen with the most expensive cloth. Always check laundering compatibility when using different fabrics together.

Fillings and trimmings

The way you line, support and insulate your bedroom and bathroom soft furnishings is as varied as the choice of the furnishing fabrics. Whether you like using man-made or natural fillings; your curtains are to be used in summer or winter; or you suffer from allergies, you are sure to be able to find a product that will suit your needs.

LINING AND INTERLINING

▲ A lining fabric performs several valuable functions – it adds weight and bulk, protects the main fabric from dust and sunlight and provides a neat back for your work. Buy 100% cotton curtain lining or plain poplin if you want a colour to match the main fabric. Use curtain lining for bed valances and behind bed heads and canopies. Interlining is used to provide bulk to curtains, sandwiched between the main fabric and the lining. Most are made from at least 95% cotton and are washable. The heaviest weight is 'bump' and the lightest 'domette' – use in place of polyester wadding if you prefer to avoid man made fibres.

THREAD

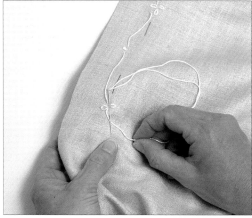

◄ Always match the washing requirements of the thread to the fabric. If you are using silk, buy silk thread; for cotton or linen, buy cotton thread. Use cotton thread for wool and a polyester/cotton mix for man made fibres – for stretchy fabrics use a polyester thread.

WADDING

◄ Polyester wadding is very light and washable, use for quilting bedcovers, pillow covers and headboards. It is available in several widths and weights – 2oz for appliqué and light quilting, 4oz for normal quilting and 8oz for bedcovers. Cotton wadding isn't washable and comes as a fluffy mixture held between thin layers of cotton or paper, use only for fine work on silk, cotton or linen.

PILLOWS AND CUSHIONS

▲ The very best pillows are filled with down from the eider duck; they are very soft, can be squashed almost to nothing and are very luxurious when compared to a feather/down mix. The price of a pillow is directly related to the quality of the filling – the best are filled with the finest down, the least expensive filled with course chicken feathers. Buy the highest down to feather ratio that you can afford. For allergy sufferers use fibre filled pillows.

TRIMMINGS

◄ Whether decorative, functional or both, always choose buttons and ribbon that fit the laundering requirements of the fabric. Most ribbons are pre-shrunk when you buy them, but as an extra precaution wash them before stitching. Attach buttons with buttonhole thread, strengthened with a dab of clear nail varnish.

DUVETS

◄ Duvets fall into the same categories as pillows. Each duvet has a 'tog' rating which is a guide to the warmth factor. A tog rating of 4.5 denotes light summer use while 13.5 – 15 is for the colder weather. Many people prefer to use a fibre filling which can be washed in a domestic machine and is kinder to allergy sufferers. During the warmer months, hang duvets out to air whenever possible, and clean every couple of years.

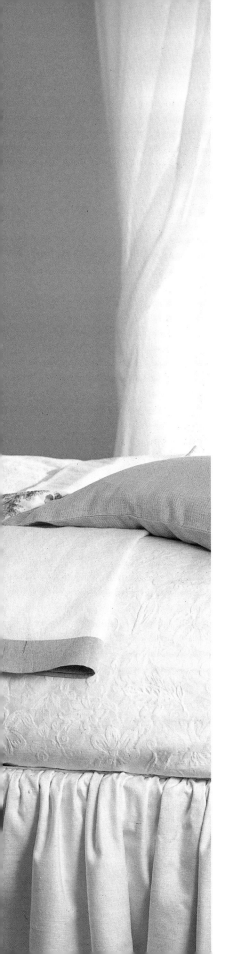

Bedroom Basics

There is nothing like sleeping in hand finished, completely individual bedding. Bed valances are always much fuller and of a better weight if you make your own; bolsters and cushions can be made to your individual requirements in size and choice of fabric.

If you are new to sewing or short of time just pick the easiest project, those who are very experienced will enjoy tackling something a little more involved. And if you feel daunted by the thought of finishing a whole bed, why not buy one set of pillow covers and make another, or decorate bought linen with appliqué and decorative stitches. This way you will still be creating your own individual look.

Decorative bed linen

If you feel you haven't the time or you are having difficulty finding wide width fabric to make your own bedding then a good alternative has to be decorating ready-made items.

You will need to choose the best quality 100% cotton, 100% linen or an equal linen and cotton mix for the best results. Timeless finishes such as appliqué, cross stitch and ribbons are ideal for decoration and can really make a difference to plain sheets and pillow cases. Choose Oxford style pillow covers which will give a reasonable stitching area and sheets with a good turn back with corded or double stitched edges.

MATERIALS:
100% cotton, 100% linen or an equal linen and cotton mix, Oxford pillow cover and sheet, embroidery thread, ribbon, matching sewing thread

FABRIC:
Ribbon embroidered pillow cover: Oxford pillow cover, enough 15mm (⅝in) ribbon to go twice around the edge of the pillow plus 25cm (10in) for each corner bow
Embroidered pillow cover and sheet: Pillow cover, sheet, 9mm (⅜in) ribbon to go once around the edge of the pillow or across the top of the sheet, embroidery thread

RIBBON PILLOW COVER

1 On an Oxford style pillow, fold ribbon over the outer edge, mitre the corners. Pin another row against the inner row of the stitching, leaving tails to tie into bows at the corners. On standard pillows, pin the ribbon on the outer edge or on the top edge of the sheet against the inner row of stitching.

2 Tack along the centre of the ribbon then machine stitch 2mm (⅛in) from the outer edges of the ribbon. Always stitch in the same direction around the pillow or across the sheet – this will stop the ribbon puckering. If using a bow, tie at the corners and stitch in place. Press.

EMBROIDERED SHEET AND PILLOW COVER

When working embroidery on sheets it is important that the stitching appears the same on the front as on the back of the sheet. Mark the positions for the knots and crosses to the fabric in a row 1cm (½in) from the stitched border, using pins to mark the centre position of the stitches.

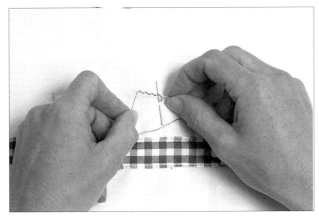

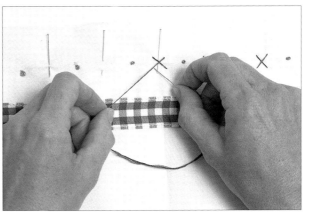

1 Using three strands of embroidery thread, work a French knot on the top of the fabric following the instructions on pages 82-85, then push the needle through to the back and make another knot.

2 The cross stitch will appear the same on both sides as long as you push the needle straight through the fabric without slanting. Keep the crosses even in size and position.

WOOL EMBROIDERED BLANKET

To spruce up the edge of a bought blanket, stitch over the manufacturer's blanket stitching with your own coloured wool. Along the edge of the blanket just inside the stitching, make an inner row of French knots and cross stitches to match the design stitched on the sheet and pillow slips. Don't worry too much about total accuracy when using embroidery to create a hand stitched finish.

Pillow covers

Bed cushions offer endless opportunities to add a splash of colour or a change of style to any bed, whilst expending the minimum of effort and cost. There can be nothing prettier than covers of floribunda roses or fresh stripes nestling among crisp white linen throughout the summer; and then at the onset of colder weather, to swap these covers for richly coloured and textured wool, plaid or velvet.

MATERIALS:
Any cotton or wool fabric – lightweight lawn for the summer or heavier richer fabric like damask, velvet or wool for the winter, matching sewing thread, seam binding for the frilled cover

FABRIC:
For each pillow: Allow two pieces of fabric 56cm wide x 76cm (22½in x 30½in) long, for a pillow size of 50cm x 70cm (20in x 28in). The finished covers should be 2cm (¾in) wider and longer than the pillow, for ease
For the tied cover: One piece of fabric 1.05m x 20cm (1⅙yd x 8in) for the facing, two pieces 10cm x 50cm (4in x 20in) for two ties
For the frilled cover: One piece 1.5m x 18cm (1⅔yd x 7in) for the frill, one piece of seam binding 2cm (¾in) wide x 1.05m (1⅙yd) long

TIED COVER

1 Make up the ties, following the instructions on pages 86-87. Place the pillow cover front and back onto the worktable with right sides together. Taking a 1.5cm (⅝in) seam allowance, pin, tack then stitch, leaving one short side open. Neaten the seams, snip across the corners then turn the cover right side out.

2 Make a 1cm (½in) hem all along one long side of the flap piece. Pin the flap around the open end of the pillow cover, holding the right sides of the fabrics together and starting at the bottom pillow cover seam. Join the short ends of the flap with a flat seam. Neaten then press flat.

3 Position one tie half way along each side. Slip each tie between the pillow cover and the flap and pin securely (for two or more ties space evenly along the sides). Stitch two rows over the ties to strengthen. Neaten then press the flap inside. Slip the cover over the pillow and knot the ties.

FRILLED COVER

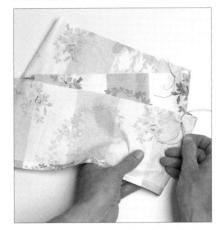  

1 Join the short ends of the frill piece to make a circle. Join using a French seam. Press under a 1cm (½in) double hem along one long edge of the frill and run a gathering thread 1.5 cm (⅝in) from the edge along the other side. Divide into four equal sections marking each with a tack. Press.

2 Join the two pillow cover pieces together following the instructions for the tied cover. Press then turn out. Stitch a marking tack half way along each side. Pin the frill around the open end of the cover with right sides of fabric together, matching the tacks on the frill to those on the cover.

3 Pull up the gathers evenly between each tack. Keep the raw edges level and pin at 1.5cm (⅝in) intervals. Machine stitch 1.5cm (⅝in) from the raw edge. Trim the seam back to 1cm (½in). Fold the binding tape over the seam and slip stitch to the stitching line on both sides.

Bed bolsters

Bed bolsters are more often for decorative than practical use, although the large ones can be most useful to prop against an uncomfortable bed head. Plain bolsters can be as useful as the very elaborate; an effective bolster need be no more than a sausage tied at both ends. Some have buttons, others piping or highly decorative finishes; however, in the end it is the mix of fabrics and colours which create the style and means to bring the simplest room to life.

MATERIALS:
Any fabric, matching sewing thread, piping, pad, card, tape

FABRIC:
Bolster piped: For a tied bolster measuring 90cm (1yd) long x 25cm (10in) diameter you will need one piece of fabric 93cm x 87cm (37in x 34½in), one piece 50cm x 24cm (20in x 10in) of fabric cut into four 50cm x 6cm (20in x 2½in) pieces for the ties, 1.8m (2yd) piping – fabric and cord see pages 88-89 for making instructions

Bolster buttoned: For a buttoned bolster measuring 90cm (1yd) long x 25cm (10in) diameter you will need one piece of fabric 120cm x 87cm (47in x 34½in), one piece 50cm x 24cm (20in x 10) cut into four 50cm x 6cm (20in x 2½in) pieces for the folded ties, circle of card 5cm (2in), circle of fabric 9cm (3½in), 1m (40in) narrow tape

Bolster knotted ends: One piece of fabric 180cm x 82.5cm (2yd x 32½in), ribbon or fabric to make the ties, see pages 86-87

BOLSTER WITH PIPED END

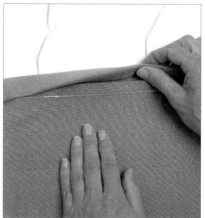

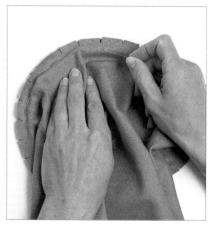

1 Snip the piping fabric edge all the way along at 1.5cm (⅝in) intervals. Pin the piping around the edge of one circle of fabric, join the piping ends. Tack and stitch the piping in place before removing the pins. Repeat with the other circle.

2 Fold the bolster fabric in half, long sides together, right side inside. Stitch 20cm (8in) from each end, 4cm (1⅝in) from the raw edges. Stitch the ties at equal distances between the openings. To neaten, fold over the seams stitching close to the fold.

3 Pin the piped circle ends to the bolster, snip to ease where necessary. Tack and stitch as close to the piping as possible. Neaten the seam, turn right side out and press. Insert the pad and tie the closures. In place of fabric ties use narrow ribbon in a contrasting colour.

BOLSTER WITH BUTTONED END

1 To make the cover, follow instruction 2 from the piped bolster on the previous page. Press under 1.5cm (⅝in) double hems at each end of the tube. Tack then stitch leaving a 2cm (¾in) opening by each side seam. Using a bodkin or safety pin, thread through each channel with narrow tape. Pull up as tightly as you can and knot the tape.

2 To make a button, cut a 5cm (2in) circle of card and a 9cm (3½in) circle of fabric. Run a row of gathering stitches around the outer edge of the fabric circle. Place the card in the centre of the fabric. Pull up the gathering threads and secure the ends. Slip stitch the button to the end of the bolster. Repeat for the other end. Insert the pad and tie the closures.

KNOTTED END

This knotted bolster cover is simple to construct from just a piece of fabric and one main seam. Neaten the ends of the tube then insert the pad before gathering up each end and knotting with a ribbon or fabric tie.

Throws

Extremely practical, wonderfully luxurious, a single throw can transform your room at a touch, and at the same time provide an extra blanket for a cold night. Bring the room alive with a splash of colour draped across the end of a bed; even change the colour from season to season. Indulge a passion for an extravagant fabric or a racy fashion colour, perhaps splash out on luxurious cashmere or shot taffeta. Crunchy linens, soft wool plaids and simple cotton checks make instantly successful throws for a country style bedroom – just fringe the ends.

MATERIALS:

Reversible woven fabric with threads loose enough to pull away to make the fringe – Scottish tartan, suiting tweed, heavy damask, rough woven cotton, linen or wool in stripes or plaids, heavyweight upholstery fabric, matching sewing thread, card

FABRIC:

Dress throw or single bedcover: You will need 2.20m (2⅜yd) x the width of the fabric 130cm (1⅜yd)
Larger bed cover: You will need 5m (5½yd) x the width of the fabric 130cm (1¾yd), cut into two 2.5m (2¾yd) lengths. Cut one in half lengthways, join this to either side of the wider piece using a flat fell seam

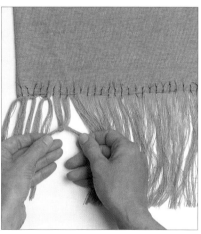

1 Pin the fabric to the worktable or hold flat with weights. Pin then tack a line 15cm (6in) from both ends across the fabric, using the fabric threads as a guide. Halfway across make a cut from the raw edge to the tacked line. Remove all the threads, one at a time, across one half width from the raw edge to the tacked line. Repeat for the other half.

2 Divide the width of fabric into 1cm – 1.5cm (⅜in – ⅝in) sections. Mark with small tacks or pins along the existing tacked line. In each section there should be roughly the same amount of threads. Take the threads from the first two sections and knot together against the fabric. Tie knots all the way across the fabric width.

3 Before tying the second row of knots, make a card gauge 6cm x 3cm (2⅜in x 1¼in). Leave the first bunch of threads untied, tie the second and the third loosely together. Hold the gauge card between this knot and the knot resting against the fabric. Correct the distance then secure the knot. Repeat across the width and on the other sides.

4 Comb out the fringe, neatening the threads so that they lie together. Place your metre rule on the fringe to hold it in place. Carefully cut away any uneven threads, with the longest and sharpest scissors you can find.

REVERSIBLE THROWS

Reversible throws can be made more substantial if you want to use them as bedcovers on a frequent basis. Choose two fabrics which are compatible for laundering and complementary in style and colour. A richly coloured wool plaid reversed with rough textured linen would be a good summer/winter combination; fringe both fabrics or just one. Throws can also be made with a plain bound edge, follow the instructions given for bedcovers on pages 38-39.

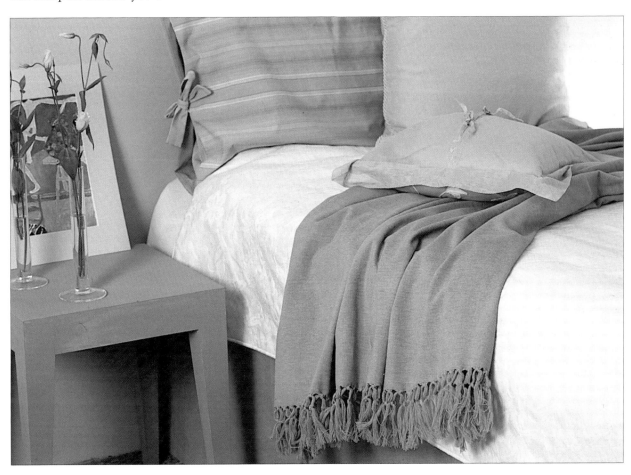

Gathered valance

Bed valances fit over the divan base and along one to four sides, depending on the style of the bed. A straight valance pleated and buttoned at the corners will finish the bed in a chic, tailored way, whilst a gathered skirt will suit a more feminine, softer look.

Almost all fabrics can be used for a valance – a solid fabric in a dark colour may be needed to 'weight' the bed or you may prefer the more delicate softer look of 'almost there' floaty organdie.

MATERIALS:
Canvas or lining fabric for the platform base, any fabric for the platform sides and skirts, matching sewing thread

FABRIC:
Platform base: Measure the bed, allowing for the width and length of the bed less 8cm (3in) extra all round. Cut and join the fabric to form the platform base
Platform edges: Cut the four platform edges adding 2cm (¾in) to all edges. Four x 2m (2¼yd) x 12cm (4¾in) strips of main fabric for platform edges
Gathered platform skirts: Make as one piece or split to fit around corner posts. Measure the skirt adding 12cm (4¾in) to the hem and 2cm (¾in) to the top and sides. Allow two and a half times around the bed for gathers

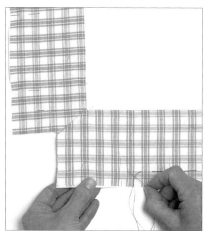

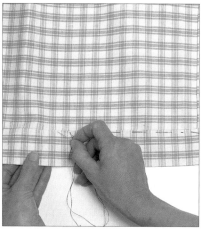

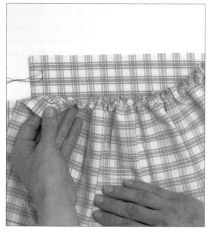

1 Press under 1.5cm (⅝in) on one long side of each of the platform edge pieces. Pin and stitch each strip to the platform base fabric. Lay the assembled base flat on the bed, cut to shape around the sides, corners or posts, adding a 2cm (¾in) seam allowance. Divide the platform edges into four sections, mark with coloured tacks.

2 Press the skirt lengths flat then join using French seams, into one long or three separate skirts. Neaten the side seams of the skirt pieces. Pin, tack then machine stitch a hem on the bottom of the skirt, working from the back and close to the folded edge. Stitch another row of machine stitches 5mm (¼in) towards the bottom of the skirt.

3 Divide each skirt into twelve equal sections, or each side into four sections, mark with coloured tacks. Run a gathering thread between each tack, 2cm (¾in) from the top edge. Pin the skirt or skirts to the platform sides, matching the corresponding tacks. Pull the gathering threads up so that the fullness lies evenly between the markers.

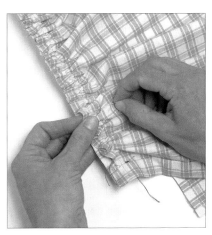

4 Pin and tack at 1.5cm (⅝in) intervals along the length, leaving the pins in to keep the gathers straight. Machine stitch making a 2cm (¾in) seam allowance, stitch again 3mm (⅛in) towards the raw edge to strengthen. Neaten the seam with an overlocker, zigzag stitches or with seam binding tape. Press towards the platform.

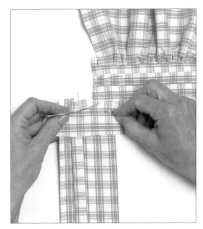

5 Turn under then stitch the top side of the platform base to neaten. If there are shaped corners, bind to neaten. Stitch 1.25cm (½in) tapes or fabric ties at each corner – these can be tied around the bed legs to hold the skirt in place. Remove all tacking stitches then press.

Straight and pleated valance

A straight bed valance with corner pleats suggests a completely different mood than the more usual gathered frill shown on page 24. The sharp tailored finish can be used to 'knock back' otherwise light, fluffy bedding and drapes, or can form the basis of a more formal treatment.

For a formal look the valance should just skim the floor; on a wooden or metal frame bed, a slightly shorter length of valance would be in keeping with the traditional country style of bed design.

MATERIALS:
Canvas or lining fabric for the platform base, any medium weight fabric heavy enough to fall along the length of the bed without sagging, lining fabric, piping, matching sewing thread

FABRICS
Platform base and edges: Measuring the bed following the instructions given on pages 78-79
Platform skirt: For these instructions the skirt will be made up in one length, falling from the sides and bottom of the bed. Measure the depth of the required valance, add 6cm (2½in) for the hems and 2cm (¾in) for the top seam. Allow approximately two widths of fabric for each side and one or two for the bottom
Platform corner flaps: The 'pleats' at each corner are neater made as separate flaps. You will need one flap for each corner 45cm – 50cm (18in – 20in) wide. Cut the flaps from the main fabric, allowing approximately two widths for the four flaps
Lining: Cut lining fabric to fit the skirt and flaps, piping

STRAIGHT AND PLEATED VALANCE

1 Make up the platform base and edges following the measuring instructions above and the making up instructions on pages 78-79. Pin the piping around the edge of the platform, snipping to ease around the corners. Tack and stitch in place before removing the pins.

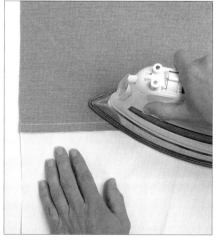

2 To line the skirt and flaps. With right sides together, pin the lining to the fabric along the lower edge. Tack and machine stitch, taking a 1.5cm (⅝in) seam allowance. Open out each piece, press the seams towards the lining. Turn the sides over 2cm (¾in) towards the wrong side, press and tack.

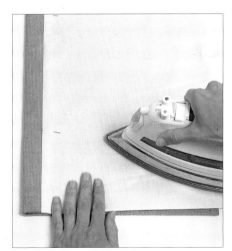

3 Fold the lining to the back, leaving 3.5cm (1½in) of the main fabric showing along the hem line. Tack along 3cm (1¼in) from the folded edge. Trim 1cm (⅜in) of the lining away at the sides. Fold under 1.5cm (⅝in) and pin so that 5mm (¼in) of the main fabric is left showing. Pin along the top edges, trim away the excess lining. Slip stitch all sides to close.

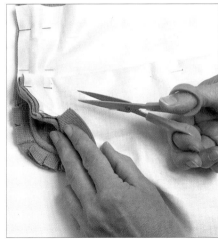

4 Pin and tack the skirt securely onto the edge of the platform. Machine stitch along the seam line. Pin the flaps around each corner, snip the seam allowance to ease. Tack and stitch close to the piping line. Stitch again all the way around just a few millimetres inside the last line. Neaten by overlocking, pinking or with seam binding. Remove the tacking and press.

PLEATED SKIRT

For a pleated skirt, decide how many pleats you would like along each side, allowing approximately 30cm (12in) extra fabric for each. Make up each skirt in the same way as for the straight bed valance. Mark the pleat positions on the platform side pieces before pinning the skirt in position, pleating the fabric as you go. Tack then machine stitch the skirt onto the valance. Neaten the seam, press.

Pin tucked cloth

Dress table cloths can be made to cover any display table, side table or dressing table from fabric which is as fine as organdie or as heavy as velvet damask. If the cloth is likely to get stained, make sure the fabric is washable, or covered with a glass top.

A simple square cloth is easy to make, small enough to launder and will disguise an old fashioned or ugly table. A pin tucked cloth does look very smart but it will take time to complete; on the other hand it is not a difficult technique to learn, and will be well worth the effort when finished.

MATERIALS:

A plain, tightly woven cotton such as lawn or organdie or a finely woven linen that falls well or silk taffeta for a special finish, matching cotton thread, embroidery thread for decoration

FABRIC:

To make a pin tucked cloth with a finished size of 1m (1¼yd) square, you will need a piece of fabric 1.24m x 1.24m (48in x 48in). Make sure that you cut the fabric exactly following the grain

1 **Cover your worktable with** a blanket or curtain lining. Place the fabric flat on your worktable. Mark the hem then the pin tuck positions along one edge of the fabric. Allow 8cm (3in) for the hem, 3cm (1¼in) gaps and 4cm (1⅜in) for each tuck. Push marking pins straight through into the worktable cover.

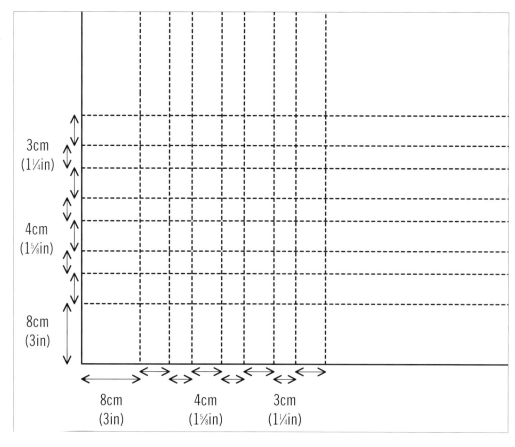

3cm (1¼in)

4cm (1⅜in)

8cm (3in)

8cm (3in)   4cm (1⅜in)   3cm (1¼in)

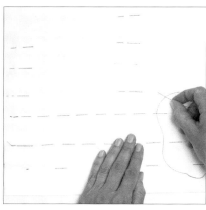

2 Tack along these lines, removing the pins as you go. Use a small ruler or cut yourself a paper marker to double check the measurements from the hem up, as you work across the row. To neaten, make a 4cm (1⅝in) double folded hem, tack then stitch close to the fold.

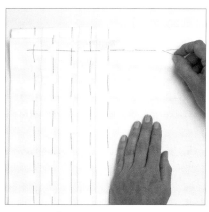

3 Pin the top two rows of tacking together, finger press along the first tuck. Pin the next eight rows of tacking to make four more tucks. Machine stitch just outside the tacking lines, to avoid catching the tacking threads. Pin and machine the tucks along the opposite side.

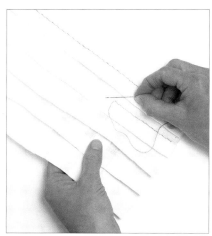

4 Repeat for the two other sides, stitching through the tucks on the finished side. Pull out the tacking threads, tie off then trim any loose ends. Press carefully, keeping the pin tucks straight. For decoration, weave embroidery thread through the top stitching line at even intervals.

Lampshades

Slip over lampshades can be used to cover an old or damaged shade, or as decoration when changing the colour scheme of a room. Card shades or very simple fabric covered frames make the best bases for fabric slip covers.

Such a small amount of lightweight fabric is needed to complete the shade, that a remnant or off cut from other furnishings projects will often work – or treat yourself to half a metre/yard of a fabric too extravagant to use for a larger job.

MATERIALS:
Lightweight fabrics, such as silk, fine linen, sprigged muslin or floral lawns that are sheer enough to let light through

FABRIC:
Measure the top and bottom circumference and the slope of your shade
For the gathered shade: Rectangle of fabric twice the bottom circumference x the length of the slope plus 14cm (5½in), 1.25cm (½in) tape – the circumference of the shade plus 2cm (¾in)
For the tied shade: Two pieces of fabric, each half the bottom circumference x the slope plus 6cm (2⅜in) and two lengths 4cm x 1m (1⅝in x 1¼yd) for the ties

GATHERED SHADE

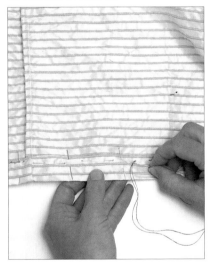

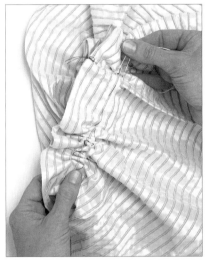

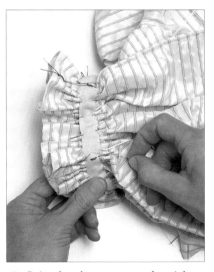

1 Join the short sides of the fabric to make a circle, using a French seam – make the seam as small as you can. Along the bottom edge, make a 3cm (1¼in) double hem to the wrong side, press then tack in place. Slip stitch through the fold line.

2 At the top edge turn over 4cm (1⅝in), press. Run two gathering threads 3cm (1¼in) and 3.5cm (1½in) from the top. Fold the cover in half and then in half again to make four sections. Mark each section with a tack. Gather the fabric cover, evenly and loosely.

3 Join the short tape ends with a 1cm (⅜in) seam, divide into four, mark with tacks. Working on the wrong side, pin the tape over the gathers. Pull up the gathers, matching the tacks. Stitch around the top and bottom of the tape. Press. Drop onto the base shade.

TIED SHADE

1 To neaten the top and bottom edge, press, tack and stitch a 1cm (⅜in) double hem along the side and the bottom edges of the two fabric pieces. Trim away the excess fabric at the corner.

2 Prepare the two folded ties without stitching, see pages 86-87. Unpin the centre sections of each tie then pin to each top edge, matching the centres. Stitch a 1cm (⅜in) seam.

3 Fold the tie over to enclose the raw edges, pin, slip stitch. Stitch the ends closed. Repeat for the other tie, press. Tie the two bows then slip the cover over the card or fabric shade.

Quilts and Covers

The bedcover is arguably the most important item in the room – it covers the largest flat area and so the colour or colours used and the style chosen will automatically predominate.

Instead of one single cover make two or three in different fabrics which can double up as comforters or throws from season to season.

When not used on the bed a throw will drape over the arm of a sofa or cover a chair; a comforter can be left at the end of the bed to be used for the cooler nights of winter.

Fabric scraps can be made into a colourful patchwork cover or a pretty throwover, but remember whatever fabric you choose it should be durable and easily washable.

This chapter contains

Duvet cover

If you haven't picked up a needle since school but want to make a contribution to your own home furnishings, then a duvet cover is the place to start. Choose stripes or checks in bright colours for a bold sporty effect; mix a floral top with a stripe underneath or choose crisp white cotton for country style. For a more sophisticated look choose soft fabrics in creams and pastels.

MATERIALS:

Washable, easy care cotton or linen, buttons, matching sewing thread, buttonhole thread

FABRIC:

Basic cover: Buy two sheets, or wide width sheeting fabric in cotton or linen. Allow 5% extra for shrinkage, wash and dry. Measure your duvet adding 5cm (2in) on each side for seams and easement. Cut a front and back, for a double cover join the fabric with French seams

Basic pillow cover: Cut the front and back pieces adding an extra 3cm (1 ¼in) for the top and side seams, and 18cm (7in) for the opening side

Buttoned cover and pillow: Cut the front and back pieces as above adding 36cm (14in) extra for the bottom hem, three buttons for each pillow, six – ten for duvet cover, buttonhole thread

Tied cover and pillow: Cut the front and back pieces as above, two pieces 130cm x 24cm (52in x 9½in) for the plackets, piping fabric 4cm (1⅝in) wide and long enough to go around the cover, six pieces 4cm x 45cm (1 ⅝in x 18in) for the fabric ties for the pillow, twelve – twenty for the duvet cover

FOR THE BUTTONED DUVET COVER

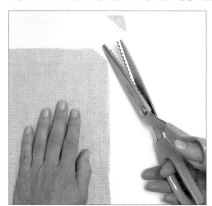

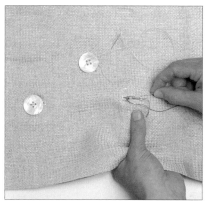

1 Place the two pieces of fabric onto the worktable, right sides facing. Pin and tack 2.5cm (1in) around the sides and top. Machine taking a 1.5cm (⅝in) seam allowance. Stitch again a short distance towards the raw edge. Trim the corners, neaten seams.

2 On the open edge, press under 24cm (9½in) to the wrong side, fold under 12cm (5½in) making a double hem. Pin, tack then machine stitch 0.5cm (¼in) from the fold line then again 1cm (½in) from the stitching line. Turn right side out, press.

3 Divide the hem width into 25cm – 30cm (10in – 12in) sections, mark with tacks. Stitch three buttonholes on the top side and buttons on the opposite side, dab the buttonhole thread with clear nail varnish. Make the pillow with a 6cm (2½in) double hem.

FOR THE TIED DUVET AND PILLOW

1 Fold the piping material in half lengthways, press. Place the top cover onto the worktable, right side up. Pin the piping onto the cover, with the raw edge 1cm (½in) from the cover edge. Stop 1cm (½in) before the corner, fold the piping back on itself to 45 degrees, continue on all sides.

2 Tack and stitch 1.5cm (⅝in) from the outside edge. Pin the under side on top, right sides together. Machine stitch inside the piping stitching line, around three sides and 20cm (8in) at each end of the opening side. Neaten. Divide the opening into 25cm – 30cm (10in – 12in) sections, stitch one tie in each.

3 Pin one placket strip each side of the opening, right sides and raw edges together. Tack and stitch just inside the piping stitching line. Fold the placket edge and ends under three times. Pin and slip stitch the inner fold to the stitching line. Turn right side out, press. Make the pillow with a 12cm (5 in) double hem.

Patchwork lined bedcover

Making a patchwork lining for a bed cover is a great way to use up all of those scraps and remnants left over from previous projects. Look out for bargain ends and take advantage of patchwork bags on sale in fabric shops.

You will just need to check that the fabric you wish to use together is compatible when laundered. Almost any combination of fabric will work, from plain blue mixed with blue checks and stripes, to a multitude of floral prints. When assembling the patches you can either work randomly or if you want a more structured design, plan before starting on paper.

MATERIALS:
Washable, easy care cotton, roughly of the same weight, piping cord, matching sewing thread

FABRIC:
Cover top: 250cm (100 in) square – one piece 5.2m x 135cm (5½yd) wide top fabric, cut to make 2 x 2.6m (3yd) lengths. Cut one in half lengthways, join the smaller pieces either side of the whole width
Interlining: One piece of sarille interlining the same size and assembled in the same way as the top fabric
Patchwork: Patchwork squares – laundered and pressed, either 441 squares x 15.5cm (6in) or 100 squares x 28cm (11in)
Piping and finishing: 1m (1¼yd) main fabric for piping, 10m (11 ½yd) piping cord, make the piping following the instructions on pages 88-89

1 Join two patchwork squares together with a 1.5cm (⅝in) flat seam. Snip away the corner at a 45 degree angle. Press flat. Continue joining squares making a 2.60m (3yd) length. Assemble all the squares in the same way. Join the lengths together to make a 2.6m (3yd) square. Press seams flat.

2 Place the top fabric onto the worktable, face down. Cut the fabric into a 256cm (102in) square. Lie the interlining over the top, matching the seams. Lock stitch with seams together. Trim the interlining sides to match the top fabric. Tack the two layers together, 1.5cm (⅝in) from the edge.

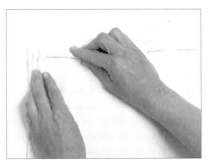

3 Turn the layers of fabric over, so that the top fabric is facing up. Pin, tack and stitch (see pages 88-89) the piping around the edge of the top fabric. Press the seam flat. If the fabric is bulky cut back the inner seam to 1cm (½in), so layering the seams. Herringbone the seam to the interlining.

4 Turn the fabric layers over, place the patchwork lining on top, matching the lining centre to the centre of the top fabric. To neaten the outer edge, finger press under 1.5 – 2cm (⅝in – ¾in) of fabric, pinning the folded edge close to the piping. Slip stitch into the piping stitching line. Press hard from the lining side, so that the seams become embedded into the interlining.

Reversible bedcover

A reversible bedcover will last a lifetime, as useful in summer as in winter. Choose a richly coloured and textured weave for the winter layer and a lighter, fresher fabric for the summer side. Tough upholstery fabrics in crunchy linen or soft woven wool can be surprisingly inexpensive and make the most lovely bedcovers. Overblown chintz partnered with wool flannel, simple cotton plaid and country tweed, rough, unbleached linen with sumptuous velvet are some of the combinations which could work very well together.

Even if nothing else in the room changes, your bedcover will enrich or lighten the whole room from season to season.

MATERIALS:
Any fabric, but the top, bottom and binding must launder the same, interlining, matching sewing thread, buttons

FABRIC:
Cover top: For a 250cm (100in) square bedcover – this is a floor length cover for a single 1m (1¼yd) bed or a valance length cover for a 150 – 180cm (60 – 72in) bed. 7.5m (8½yd) of fabric at least 110cm (45in) wide, cut into twenty five x 55cm (22in) squares
Cover bottom: 5m x 130cm (5½yd x 52in) wide fabric, cut into two lengths 2.5m (2¾yd) long. Cut one in half lengthways and join to either side of the full width piece
Interlining: 5m x 130cm (5½yd x 52in) wide interlining, assemble as cover bottom
Finishing: To make 7.5cm (3in) binding from 180cm x 130cm (72in x 52in) wide fabric, cut nine x 20cm (8in) pieces across the width, join to make one long length with flat seams, 32 buttons approximately 2cm (¾in) in diameter

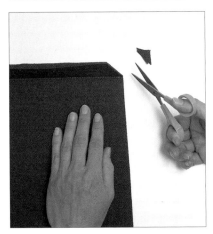

1 For the cover top join the fabric squares together in lengths of five, making 2.5cm (1in) flat seams. Press. Snip away the corners at a 45 degree angle.

2 Join two lengths together, pinning the seam joins exactly. Tack, keeping the pins in at each seam junction. Machine stitch 2.5cm (1in) flat seams. Join the other lengths in the same way. Remove tacking threads, press.

3 Lay the interlining onto the worktable. Place the assembled bedcover top over this, right side up, leaving an equal border of interlining all around. Pin then tack across the centre and 2cm (¾in) from the outside edge.

4 With right sides together pin on the border. Start at the top, approximately 30cm (12in) from one corner. At the corner, fold the binding back on itself, leaving a folded flap which will be 7.5 cm (3in) after the seams have been stitched. Tack as far as the seam allowance before the flap, fold the flap over and continue to pin along the next side, keeping the seam allowance exact.

5 Continue until you have covered all sides, join the ends of the binding with a flat seam. Stitch using your machine plate as a guide 2.5cm (1in) from the raw edges. At each corner, stitch right up to the flap, back stitch then lift the needle. Fold the flap over and continue to stitch along the next side. Press the binding from the front then mitre the corners neatly.

6 Turn the cover top over. Onto this place the bottom lining fabric, tack to the front and interlining, inside the stitching line. These tacking stitches will remain. Fold the binding over to the lining, keeping the fold 7.5cm (3in) wide and tight to the raw edges. Fold the under corners to mitre the opposite way to those on the top. Press hem under so that the fold lines up with the stitching line. Tack, then slip stitch with small stitches. Remove all tacking then press. Stitch buttons at each corner.

Quilted comforter

Quilting is an attractive and practical way to sandwich extra warmth between two layers of fabric, adding interest to the bed, and an extra cover on a cool night. On antique covers and eiderdowns we can see the most intricate quilting patterns and stitches, which must have taken hours and hours of dedicated working.

For those with limited time and expertise, a simple machine stitched cover quilted in channels can be quite effective. Hand stitching larger quilts might be the best option – it can be quite difficult to fit a very large quilt under the machine arm.

MATERIALS:

Any fabric can be used – if you want to machine stitch the channels choose a fine fabric so that the cover will roll up tightly. If you want to hand stitch, the fabric should not be too tough or the stitching will soon become laborious and uncomfortable, piping cord, matching threads

FABRIC:

Cover: For a quilt measuring 150cm x 200cm (60in x 80in) you will need two pieces of fabric 184cm x 224cm (74in x 90in), three pieces x 4oz polyester wadding 172cm x 210cm (64in x 84in), 7.50m (8½yd) piping cord or made up frill

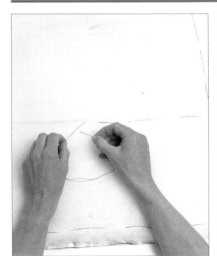

1 Place the top fabric onto the worktable, right side down. Pin the corners to the table surface, over this lay the polyester wadding. Pin and tack 2cm (¾in) from the outer edges and from the centre point to each edge. Machine around the outside, 1.5cm (⅝in) from the raw edges. Turn the fabric and wadding over.

2 Pin and stitch the piping along the outer seam line, clipping and easing the piping at the corners as you work around the cover, see pages 88-89. If you have chosen a frilled edge, make up a frill, see making a frilled pillow cover on page 19. Stitch the frill in place instead of or as well as the piping.

3 On top place the bottom fabric piece, pin around three sides close to the piping. Tack and stitch around the top and sides. Trim the corners and wadding to 1.5cm (⅝in) on all sides. Turn right side out, press. Fold under the seam allowance on the bottom edge and slip stitch to close.

4 Tack the five layers together, vertically 10cm (4in) from the sides and horizontally every 40 – 50cm (16 – 20in). These tacking lines are to stop the fabric moving, while you quilt. Along the top edge, divide the cover into channels – 23cm (9in) from each side with 21cm (8½cm) gaps between. Pin the same across the centre and along the bottom edge. Mark the stitching channels onto the fabric by joining the lines with a long ruler and soft pencil. Tack the length of the cover, 1.5cm (⅝in) either side of each line. Roll up the cover and machine stitch along each pencilled line, starting at the top and working down. Remove all tacking, neaten and trim any loose ends.

HAND STITCHING

You may prefer to hand stitch the quilting lines in patterns such as diamonds or interlocking circles. It doesn't really take that much longer to stitch as long as you tack all of the lines firmly before stitching. Most designs are best set within a border, so mark out 15 – 20cm (6-8in) on the outside of your quilt, working a design of circles or squares within.

Tufted comforter

Comforters are useful extra bedding, and this one especially quick to make; just a bought duvet sandwiched between top and bottom covers. Hand made tufts of wool, cotton or chenille are stitched through top and bottom to hold the layers together.

Almost any fabric can be used and it can be fun to choose different fabric for the bottom and top. Crunchy denim and Madras checks, or gingham and brushed cotton are good combinations for teenagers and children; roughly woven linen reversed with a primitive stripe for the country look; or try velvet mixed with wool for a more unusual combination.

MATERIALS:
Any fabric can be used, depending only on how much you will be washing the cover, single duvet 4.5 – 7.00 tog rated for the summer, 10.5 – 15 for the winter, wool or linen thread for the tufts, matching sewing thread

FABRIC:
Top cover: Fabric cut to size 124cm x 204cm (50in x 82in) - measurements are for a single comforter size 120cm x 200cm (48in x 80in)
Bottom cover: Fabric size 114cm x 184cm (45in x 74in)
Filling: Single duvet 135cm x 200cm (53in x 80in)
Tufts: Wool or linen thread

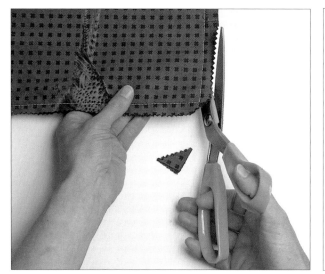

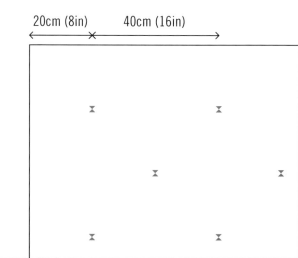

1 Place both pieces of fabric onto the worktable and pin, right sides together. Tack around the sides and top. Stitch 2cm (¾in) seams on the three tacked sides, and then just 20cm (8in) from each corner of the fourth side. Trim the corners, neaten the seam. Turn right side out, press.

2 To mark the buttoning positions, first divide the cover into squares of 40cm (16in), leaving 20cm (8in) around the edges. Whatever size cover you are making try to keep the squares roughly to this size. Mark with pins and then with marking tacks on both sides of the cover.

3 To make the tufts, cut a piece of card 3cm (1¼in) wide and a length of wool 130cm (50in). Cut a hole 0.75 cm (⅜in) wide from the middle to the end of the card. Wind the wool around the card tightly and evenly over the hole. Cut another length of wool 20cm (8in) long and tie around the centre of the tuft, pull tightly. Knot and tie twice. Make 46 tufts.

4 Fill the cover with the duvet. Shake to make sure the duvet reaches right into the corners. Pin at each corner. Slip stitch the opening closed. Stitch one tuft on a marking tack, push the needle right through the duvet, coming out on the marking tack below, stitch another tuft in place. Fasten securely and repeat with the other tufts.

Patchwork cover

Children love to have their own bedcover – so they can snuggle up in it while playing games on the floor! It will probably be taken in the car on holiday, into the garden and to a friend's house, so it will need to be durable and washable. Instead of one of the popular children's characters or fashion colours, try deep tones of the primaries – blue, green or red. Choose traditional topics such as animals, alphabet letters or numbers which are timeless and will last for years.

MATERIALS:
The top, under and binding fabrics should all be of the same weight and fibre content. Coloured denims, brushed cotton, twill, wool flannel would all be suitable, matching sewing thread, wool thread, tapestry needle

FABRIC:
Single cover: Fabric A – six pieces 47cm x 35cm (18½in x 13¾in) and two pieces 47cm x 109cm (18½in x 43in), fabric B – seven pieces 47cm x 35cm (18½in x 13¾in), fabric C – two pieces 40cm x 47cm (16¾in x 18½in) – measurements are for a single cover 132cm x 234cm (52in x 92in)
Lining: Fabric cut to size 138cm x 240cm (54½in x 94½in)
Finishing: Wool thread for blanket stitching

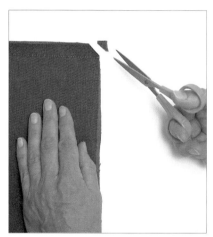

1 Join the fabrics together as shown in the diagram. Pin and stitch with flat 1.5cm (⅝in) seams. It is extremely important that the seams are all exactly the same size. Use an invisible pen to mark the seam line, or use the machine plate as your guide. The end of each seam should be trimmed to a 45 degree angle and pressed flat.

2 Join the five rows separately and then join row 1 to row 2 and so on until the whole area is stitched together. Match the seams and pin through the centre of both. Pin to each side so that the join will hold firm. Pin all the seams and then between. If there is any fullness, ease carefully. Tack, but keep the pins in. Stitch 1.5cm (⅝in) seams.

3 Press all seams flat. Place the lining onto the worktable, right side down. Over this place the joined top fabric. Pin around the sides. Trim both fabrics so that the top is 132cm x 234cm (52in x 92in) exactly and the lining is 4cm (1⅝in) larger. Tack around the outer edge and across the centres vertically and horizontally.

4 Fold the lining over onto the top fabric. Turn under the raw edges of the border making it just under 2cm (¾in). Mitre the corners and tack in place. Sew large blanket stitch over the border edge using a wool thread, see pages 82-85. This will hold the fabrics together and finish the edge.

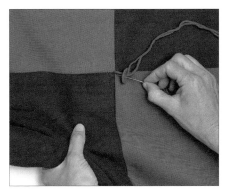

5 Using wool thread stitch buttons onto the cover where the rectangles intersect, double stitch through both layers, making a double knot to finish. Tie off securely then cut the wool thread leaving short ends. Instead of wool you could use a narrow tape or brightly coloured ribbon.

FABRIC PLACEMENT

Join the fabric pieces together following the diagram below.

A	B	A
B	A	B
	C	
A	B	A
B	A	B
A	B	A

Bedheads and Canopies

Canopies dress not just the bed, but the whole room. A single length of fabric slung over two very basic bamboo poles can have a dramatic effect on the whole room. A four poster bed frame, structurally very beautiful but sometimes a little hard, can be softened remarkably with a length of muslin draped over the top half.

Filmy muslin and fine linen make great summer drapes; keep them for the winter too, but add another layer outside of coloured taffeta or a wool plaid to make the bed feel richer and warmer.

If you prefer a minimal look, straight lengths of fabrics in country stripes or vibrant silks can be tied to each post and then loosened slightly to canopy over.

Buttoned cover

You will need to have an existing headboard under this smart buttoned cover. It can be old, new, wooden, metal or fabric covered, but the top needs to be square so that the padded cover can wrap over neatly. Perfect for children as the cover is squashy and comfortable, and can easily be slipped off and popped in the washing machine.

The inside is made from a bought duvet; the outer fabric can be plain or patterned, but should be washable.

MATERIALS:
Any washable fabric – cotton, denim or brushed cotton, single duvet - 4.5 tog, toggles or buttons – wooden, leather, fabric covered or of any material that will withstand washing, buttonhole thread, matching sewing thread, staple gun

FABRIC:
Bedhead cover: For a bedhead 100cm (40in) wide x 60cm (24in) high you will need two pieces of fabric 118cm (46in) wide x 140cm (55in) long, single duvet – 4.5 tog, six toggles or buttons
Bedhead – other sizes: To find the correct fabric size, add 18cm (7in) to the width and twice the height plus 20cm (8in), the duvet should be the width of the headboard x twice the height
Headboard: If you don't have a bedhead, buy a piece of 20mm (1in) board the width of the bed x 60cm (24in) high, paint or cover with fabric then fit to the bed.

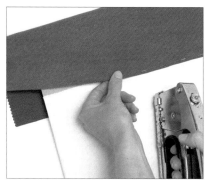

1 Cover the headboard with lining fabric, using a stapler or small tacks to hold it in place. Cover the side edges of the board with strips of the main fabric, this should be folded then slipped over the edges of the board. Staple or tack in place. Alternatively paint the headboard with emulsion paint, so that when the sides are buttoned together the bare wood will not show between the buttons.

2 Cut the two pieces of fabric to size, press and lay flat. Place the two fabrics on the worktable, right sides together, with any pattern running top to bottom. Pin and tack all around, leaving an opening approximately 60cm (24in) wide along the bottom. Stitch all around, leaving the opening and allowing 1.5cm (⅝in) seams. Neaten the seam. Press.

3 Cut the duvet to the width of the headboard and twice the height plus 20cm (8in). Finish the cut edges using an overlocker or a machine zig zag stitch. Place the duvet centrally onto the fabric, pin the top edge to the seam line and the bottom edges together. Stitch along the top just inside the stitching line and along the bottom edge 1cm (⅜in) in.

4 Turn right sides out, pushing a point turner into the corners to keep them square. Slip stitch the hole to close. Pin the sides together 6cm (2¼in) in from the seams, keeping the duvet inside the pinned line. Tack the line firmly, and top stitch the length with buttonhole thread.

5 Fold the bedhead cover in half, pinning the sides together. Mark positions for three buttons along each side. Make buttonholes on the front piece following the instructions with your machine. Stitch buttons to correspond. Slip the cover over the bedhead and button up the sides.

Slip cover bedhead

Wooden and metal bedheads always look good, but are not at all comfortable if you like to sit up in bed for Sunday breakfast or to read. A pile of pillows propped up against the back is one answer, but another is to make your own headboard from MDF which you can then pad and cover with a tied slip cover made from a pretty fabric.

MATERIALS:

Any closely woven cotton, linen, silk or wool can be used – washable for easy care, lining fabric, piping to fit round the edge, ribbon ties, seam tape, foam, wadding and lining fabric to pad the headboard, matching sewing thread, paper for template, pencil, sticky tape, staple gun, PVA glue

FABRIC:

Cover front: For a bedhead 100cm (40in) wide x 60cm (24in) deep, one piece of main fabric 110cm x 70cm (44in x 28in), piping to go up the sides and over the top of the cover

Cover back: One piece of lining fabric 115cm x 70cm (46in x 28in), border edge for the lining fabric – two pieces of main fabric 8cm x 64cm (3⅛in x 25in) for the sides, one piece 100cm x 22cm (40in x 9in) for the top

Side opening: four 10cm x 50cm (4in x 20in) plackets, eight 30cm (12in) lengths of ribbon, eight 50cm (20in) lengths of white seam tape

Headboard covering: 5mm (¼in) foam 110cm x 70cm (44in x 28in), 2oz polyester wadding 110cm x 70cm (44in x 28in), two pieces of lining fabric 110cm x 70cm (44in x 28in)

1 Lay the wooden headboard on top of the foam, cut around the outer edge. Spread PVA glue over the front side of the headboard, attach the foam. Staple 2-3mm (⅛in) in from the edge of the board. Lay the headboard foam side down on the wadding, cut around the outer edge. Repeat for the lining fabric adding enough fabric to fold onto the reverse side of the board. Lay the wadding over the foam, onto this place the lining fabric, pin both layers to the foam. Turn the headboard over. Fold the excess lining fabric to the reverse side of the board and staple. Cut a piece of lining fabric to cover the exposed central area of the board. Fold the edges over and staple to the board.

2 Make a paper template of the headboard back and one of the front extended to include the top and side edges of the board. Both should have a seam allowance on all sides. Cut a front from the main fabric using the larger template; a back from the lining fabric using the smaller template; and three border edge pieces from the main fabric. These should be tacked then stitched to the top and side edges of the back lining fabric.

3 Lay the front cover fabric over the headboard, make small darts at the top corners where the fabric extends over the edges of the board. Pin, tack then machine stitch the piping around the sides and top of the front cover fabric matching the raw edges.

4 With right sides of fabric together, pin and tack the back cover over the front. Leave an opening on both sides, this will need to be the length of the side placket pieces. Machine stitch along the tacking line, following the edge of the cover and just inside the previous stitching line.

5 Pin the ribbon ties, in pairs, to either edge of the side openings against the piping. Repeat for the other side. Pin and stitch a placket strip to one of the four opening edges, with right sides together and over the ribbon ties. Press each strip into three, enclosing the raw edges within. Slip stitch along the length. Attach ties along the bottom edge. Neaten the bottom edge and seams. Tie the cover onto the headboard.

Muslin curtains

Mosquito nets are mostly bought to keep the bugs away to ensure a good nights sleep – but with a little work this same muslin netting can make a good, inexpensive bed canopy. The muslin should be fixed securely to the ceiling or wall; this can done with a small hook. Decorate the fabric to suit your own style of room with ribbon roses, bows or if you like to work with paints, make your own stencil and add floral bunches, borders or even some summer wildlife to the muslin.

Or to soften a four poster bed, drape muslin over the frame and leave to fall in soft folds around the bed.

MATERIALS:

Muslin, fine cotton, organdie, organza or gingham are all suitable fabrics which are inexpensive enough to be able to buy in quantity, ribbon, wire edge ribbon, matching sewing thread, hook for wall or ceiling, cord or string, paper, pencil

FABRIC:

To hang the net 250cm (100in) high, and for a bed size of 150cm x 200cm (60in x 80in), you will need to buy sixteen lengths of 2.70m (3yd) to give three times the fullness, two x 3m (3⅓yd) lengths of 15mm – 20mm (⅝in – ¾in) ribbon, twelve x 1.5m (1⅔yd) lengths of 40mm – 50mm (15½in – 20in) wire edge ribbon, wall or ceiling hook, cord or string for hanging curtain, white paper for the template 1.5m (1⅔yd) x the width of the border edge

MAKING ROSES

1 Bunch the ends of the muslin lengths together and tie securely to a ceiling or wall hook. Drape the muslin around the bed and leave to fall in soft folds. To make the ribbon roses, run a gathering thread along one side of each length of plain ribbon, pull up the thread and then wind up the ribbon lengths to make 'roses'.

2 Secure the gathering thread before stitching the ribbon layers together at the gathered end. Make a selection of different colours, sizes and styles of rose. Full roses will result when both gathering and winding is looser: smaller, tighter roses will be formed with tighter gathering and winding.

3 Stitch the roses in groups, randomly all over the muslin canopy. Mix the colours and sizes of the roses within each bunch. Using a long length of wire edged ribbon, tie a large bow. Stitch the bow to the top of the muslin over the bunched fabric. Add a few roses around the ribbon bow.

WAVY BORDER EDGE

1 Concertina fold the white paper, draw a wavy shape on the front side. Cut along the drawn line and unfold the paper. This is your paper template for cutting the fabric. Pin the paper template to the border muslin, cut out a length of muslin following the template lines. Remove the template and re-attach it further along the fabric. Keep attaching and cutting until the complete length of border edge muslin has been cut. Pin the border edge to the main curtain, right sides together. Machine stitch along the outside edge.

2 Turn the curtain and border right side out. Press the border flat to the curtain, pin along the flat edge and the inside wavy edge of the muslin border. Zig zag machine stitch along the length of the wavy edge. Remove the pins, press. Drape the muslin curtain over the back of a four poster bed to soften the bed without making too much of a statement.

Pintucked curtains

Often the most effective furnishings are those which are breathtaking in their simplicity. Curtains in soft, filmy textures make inexpensive, stylish bed curtains, made simply with just machined or hand stitched sides and hems.

A good fabric with an interesting texture, finished with tiny pintucks, or decorated with pearl buttons, elegant in understatement, might be hung with the finest rouleau ties or buttoned tabs.

MATERIALS:
Any light and filmy fabric with a straight grain and fairly tightly woven to hold finger pressed pin-tucks – muslin, linen scrim, fine cotton lawn, organdie or organza, matching sewing thread

FABRIC:
Curtains: Four lengths of fabric 130cm (52 in) wide x length plus 16cm (6in) for the hem
Curtain finishing: Four strips of fabric 4cm (1⅝in) wide x 80cm (32in) for the top binding, forty eight folded ties (see pages 86-87) finished length 50cm (20in), cut the fabric for each tie four times the width and 3cm (1⅛in) longer than the finished tie

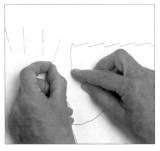

1 To mark the pintucks, measure, pin and tack at 2cm (¾in) intervals all along the top edge. Do the same again 30cm (12in) from the top. If you are making a V shape with the pintucks, pin again 55cm (22in) from the top. At regular intervals, measure back to the selvedge to check that you are keeping straight.

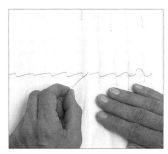

2 Leave 4cm (1⅝in) at the edge, then pleat the next 2cm (¾in) in half to make the first pintuck. Pin along the length to 30cm (12in). Pleat together each alternative 2cm (¾in) all across the width, leaving 4cm (1⅝in) at the other end. For the V shaped design, follow the illustration and pin 30-55cm (12-22in) lengths onto the fabric. Tack each pleat.

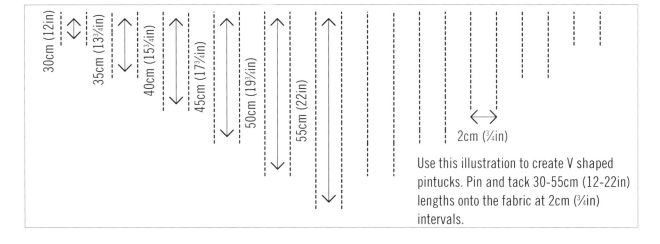

Use this illustration to create V shaped pintucks. Pin and tack 30-55cm (12-22in) lengths onto the fabric at 2cm (¾in) intervals.

3 Machine stitch the pintucks using the machine plate as a guide and keeping the needle just inside the tacked line. Remove the tacking threads and press the pintucks in the same direction. Make then slip stitch a 2cm (¾in) double hem on both long sides and a 8cm (3in) double hem along the bottom of each curtain. Pin and tack the binding length along the top edge. If necessary neaten the top edge. Stitch the binding 1cm (½in) from the raw edge.

4 Pin twelve folded ties, at the back of each curtain, in pairs, at approximately 12cm (4½in) intervals. Stitch the ties securely, zig zagging from the stitched line out towards the raw edge. Press from the front. Fold the binding over and then fold in half to enclose the raw edges. Turn the sides in and slip stitch along the back, stitching into the machined stitches.

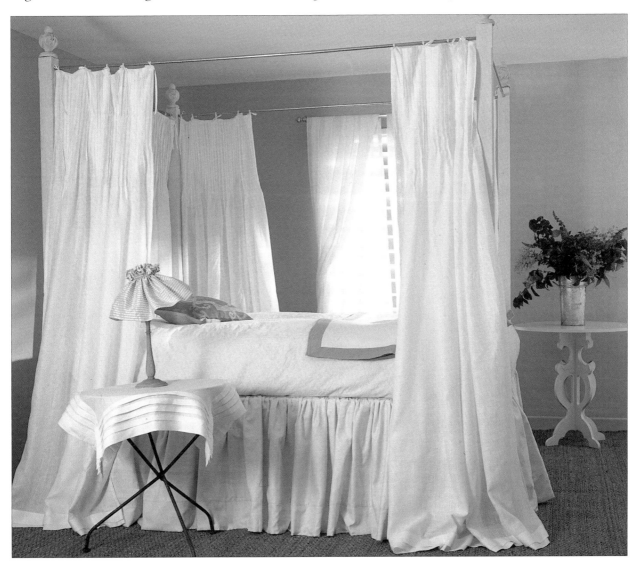

Tied bed curtains

Four poster bed frames were designed originally to hold thick, heavy curtains so that, with no room heating, once in bed you stayed warm and cosy. Tapestry hangings and heavy rugs were the commonplace, hung at each corner to pull closed on all four sides. Happily, in this day and age, the bed can be decorated for pleasure rather than necessity. Even so, curtains should be full enough to meet if and when pulled, or the drapes will look rather half hearted. Simple curtains in silk, cotton or linen can look quite exquisite when finished with a little hand stitching.

MATERIALS:
Almost any light to medium weight fabric, silk woven to look like linen has been used for this project, matching sewing thread, embroidery thread

FABRIC:
Eight lengths of fabric 130cm (52in) wide x the length from the top bar to the floor plus any extra allowance, adding 16cm (6in) for the hem, 8cm (3in) for the heading. 60 strips of fabric 10cm x 45cm (4in x 18in) for the ties, 30 strips of fabric 10cm x 45cm (4in x 18in) for the side ties

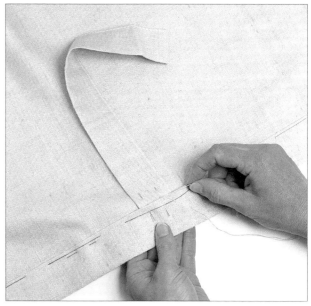

1 Place one curtain length onto the worktable, right side down. Press the side edges and the top 8cm (3in) to the wrong side. Press under again to make 4cm (1⅝in) seams, pin. Press the bottom 16cm (6in) to the wrong side. Depending on the thickness of the fabric, fold or mitre the corners. Make-up the ties (see page 86), folding 1cm (½in) on each side to make the ties 4cm (1⅝in) wide.

2 Unfold the side seams and hem, pin the ties so that each is 6cm (2in) inside the fold line. Position five pairs of ties along the heading, 8cm (3in) from each side seam, with equal distances between. Position three more ties down the side. These should be spaced 30cm (12in), 60cm (24in) and 90cm (36in) from the top. Pin and tack the seams enclosing the ties.

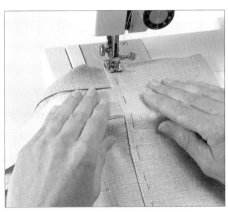

3 As the curtains will be tied together in pairs, half will need ties on the right hand side and half on the left. Stitch each tie to the inner fold line of the seam. Re-fold the turnings and tack around all edges.

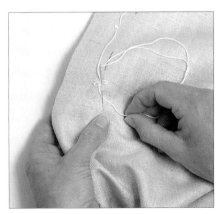

4 To finish the side seams and hem, stitch a simple embroidery design around all the edges in detached chain stitch, running stitch and French knots. The stitches should be neat enough to be seen from both sides of the curtain.

Four poster canopy

Four poster beds are structurally pleasing in their own right, so often they are lavishly draped and curtained covering the beauty of their shape and frame. A much more minimal treatment will leave a clear, airy, open feel to the bed. Plain coloured, structured, bed linen continues the theme.

Checks and flowers refresh memories of summer days lying in the garden; a quick change to covers and pillows in chenille and wool evokes the atmosphere of winter evenings in front of a burning fire. A canopy really is just a framework for the rest of the bedding – choose an undemanding fabric for an easy change of mood.

MATERIALS:
Any fabric, but cottons and linens wash and drape well. If you want to use a thick fabric for the main canopy, use a medium weight fabric for the binding, matching sewing thread

FABRIC:
Small bed frame: For a frame size 100cm x 200cm (40in x 80in) you will need, two x 1.50m (1⅔yd) and one x 2m (2¼yd) of 100cm (40in) wide main fabric
Small bed edging fabric: 6cm (2in) wide strips – six x 1.80m (2yd), four x 2.30m (2⅔yd) and two x 2.80m (3¼yd).
Large bed frame: For a frame size 200cm x 200cm (80in x 80in) you will need, four x 1.50m (1⅔yd) and two x 2m (2¼yd) of 130cm (52in) wide main fabric
Large bed edging fabric: 6cm (2in) wide strips – eight x 2.80m (3¼yd) and four x 2.30m (2⅔yd)

1 Join the fabric with French seams, for the double bed - the half widths should be either side of a full width centre panel. Cut the edging fabric into 6cm (2in) strips. Join the 6cm (2in) strips into lengths, each should be 80cm (32in) longer than the side to which it will be stitched.

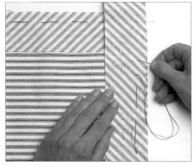

2 Place the top canopy section onto the worktable, right side up. Along each side pin one of the corresponding edging strips, right side down, so 40cm (15½in) projects out from each end. Tack and stitch 1.5cm (⅝in) from the edge, stopping 1.5cm (⅝in) from the corner.

3 Fold over the edging strips so that 1.5cm (⅝in) remains on the front, press from the front. From the back, fold in half again so that there is also a 1.5cm (⅝in) binding on the back and the fold line is in line with the stitching line. Snip a 1.5cm (⅝in) square out of each corner.

4 Fold the 40cm (15½in) ends into four to make ties 1.5cm (⅝in) wide. Fold the raw ends inside and pin. Slip stitch along each side to close the ties and along the canopy, stitching in to the previous stitches. If you prefer you can machine stitch the ties closed and slipstitch the binding.

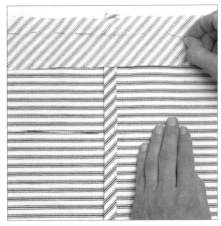

5 Repeat with the other two sections. You may want to add extra ties at intervals, depending on the design of your bed. Stitch any extra ties firmly to the space between the raw edges and the stitching line at the end of step 2. Tie the canopy to the bed frame.

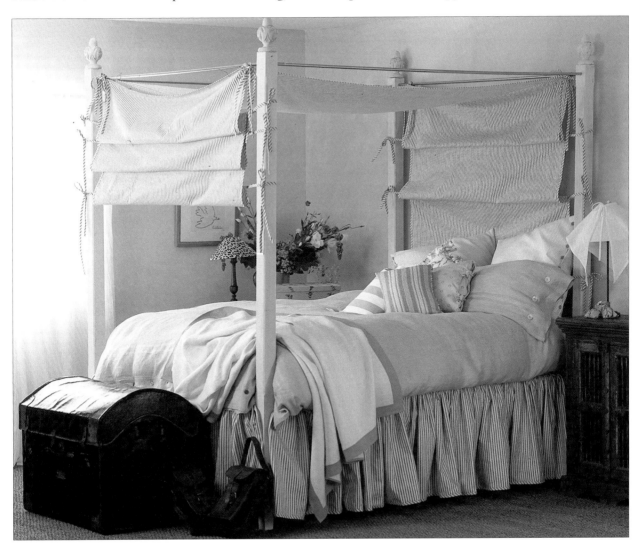

Over bed canopy

A simple and effective way to furnish a room is to drape a canopy over the bed. Slung over poles which have been hung from the ceiling, a canopy can be lowered or raised at will. A high ceiling can be visually lowered, uninteresting decoration rejuvenated. For those constantly on the move or awaiting a redecoration programme, a simple canopy can be a valued asset. Poles can be gilded wood with fantastic finials, or just basic bamboo bean poles: all that is needed to keep the whole apparatus in the air are some lengths of cord and hooks.

MATERIALS:
Any double sided cotton fabric in stripes, checks, florals, such as lawn or ticking, matching sewing thread

FABRIC:
Main fabric 130cm (52in) x 4m (4⅓yd), binding fabric 1.50m (1⅔yd) cut on the cross into 8cm (3in) wide strips

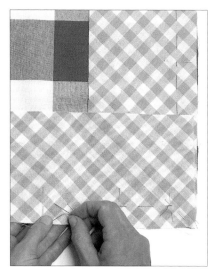

1 Cut the binding fabric on the cross into 8cm (3in) wide strips. Pin and stitch the strips of fabric together to make an 11m (12yd) length of binding fabric. Cut the remaining strips down to make eight x 6cm (2½in) x 60cm (24in) strips for the folded ties. Make up the ties following the instructions on page 86. Pin the binding fabric onto the main fabric along all four sides.

2 To make the binding sit neatly around the corners, make a folded mitre. Finger press the excess corner binding material at a 45 degree angle, fold the flap onto the binding and then back the other way onto the binding, checking that it is flat against the outer edge of the fabric in both directions. Tack the binding onto the main fabric 2cm (¾in) from the raw edges.

3 Following the tacking line, machine stitch the binding onto the edge of the main fabric, stopping as you meet each corner flap and starting again on the other side – this will create a neat finish at the corners. Pin the ties in pairs, with raw edges together on the edge of the main fabric, 150cm (60in) from one end and 50cm (20in) from the other on both sides.

4 Press from the right side of the fabric. Fold the binding to the back, keeping an exact 2cm (¾in) width all around the canopy. Fold the corner flaps to the right on the top and to the left at the back.

5 On the reverse side of the fabric, fold under the binding fabric to make a 2cm (¾in) wide edging. Pin and tack the binding to the main fabric then slip stitch to the machine stitched line.

Scalloped corona

Corona curtains are usually held by a coronet shaped circlet above the bed, draping to either side of the bed or sweeping around the back and to the sides.

Lighter than a four poster and less intrusive than an over bed canopy, a corona can be hung with two or three layers of floaty, see-through fabric which can be left to hang in folds around the bed. The sides can be turned back and adorned with ribbons or roses, hand embroidered or finished with a scalloped edge of creamy picot lace.

MATERIALS:

Any light floaty see-through fabric, organdie, organza, muslin, fine cotton lawn, fine linen, lining fabric, corona, deep heading curtain tape, picot lace, embroidery thread, matching sewing thread, medium weight white card for the template, pencil

FABRIC:

Two, three or four lengths of main fabric each 130cm (52in) wide x 2.50m (2¾yd), same amount of lining fabric, 8m (9 yd) picot lace, 2cm (¾in) deep heading curtain tape 3m – 6m (3¼yd – 6¾yd)

1 Fix the corona to the wall approximately 2.4m (94in) from the floor. If you have very high ceilings you may want to fix the corona higher than this. Measure from the fitting position to the floor, allow for the length of the curtain, adding 4cm (1⅝in) for the hem and heading. Two lengths will be needed if the drape is to hang either side of the bed, three if the drape will hang around the back of a single bed and four for a double bed. Join the lengths of main and lining fabric with flat seams.

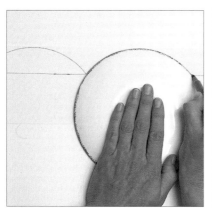

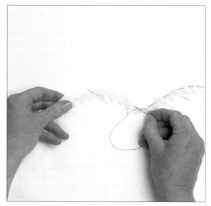

2 On medium weight card 60cm (24in) x 6cm (2½in), draw a line 3cm (1¼in) from one long edge. Position a saucer centrally on the line. Draw around the curve. Repeat along the card, cut out the template.

3 Pin the template on the edge of the fabric and draw around the shapes. Start at the top of each side, work down and along the hem towards the back. Cut out the scalloped fabric edge along the drawn line.

4 Pin, tack and stitch the lace edge to the right side of the fabric, 1cm (½in) from the cut edge. The lace should be pointing towards the centre of the fabric, so that when the curtain is turned the lace will face outwards.

5 With the curtain flat on the worktable and with right sides together, pin and tack the lining to the curtain, 15cm (6in) from the outer edge. Pin around the scallops and at the heading. Stitch together, following the shaped edge, just inside the previous stitching line. Trim around the shaping, snip into each point.

6 Turn the canopy right sides out. Press the scalloped edge – easing the fabric to make the best shapes. Press the heading 4cm (1⅜in) to the outer side. Pin the heading tape just over 2cm (¾in) from the folded edge, covering the raw edge. Tack and stitch the tape to the fabric. For added detail, work embroidery stitches along the scalloped edge.

Bathroom Accessories

Bathrooms are often neglected areas when it comes to soft furnishings, as all the attention is focused on the hard surfaces. The projects in this chapter are all useful and easy to make in an evening or a few hours. Fabrics can be chosen to match the colour scheme of an adjoining bedroom, or use simple checks and stripes which complement the overall style of your home. Pre-shrunk cottons and linens are the most suitable fabrics – look out for towelling remnants, tea towels and napkins which could be used separately or joined in squares for linen bags and shower curtains.

A simple cushion, see bed cushions page 20, can be made for a headrest at the end of the bath, or to soften a hard stool seat. Curtains around a shower or bath look elegant, but the fabric will need to be able to take steam without fear of shrinkage. Line with a bought, plain waterproof curtain to protect your fabric.

Fabric covered boxes look especially good in neat piles, keeping the bathroom tidy and holding any amount of things which you might prefer not to have on show.

This chapter contains

Shower curtains

Whilst it is easy to find bright, fun, ready-made shower curtains for a pool or for a child's room, curtains designed to discreetly blend in with more subtly coloured shower rooms can be difficult to find. The answer is to make your own. The best solution is to have two layers – an inner, waterproof curtain and an outer curtain made in a fabric to match your bedroom or bathroom scheme.

MATERIALS:
Washable outer fabric, shower-proof inner fabric or plain ready-made shower curtain, metal pole bent to fit your shower area, eyelet set, matching sewing thread, checked ribbon

FABRIC:
Curtain: For both the inner and outer fabrics, measure the pole length and to the floor, you will need approximately one and a quarter times fullness, allow 4cm (1⅝in) for each side seam, 10cm (4½in) for the heading and the hem. Usually one width of fabric is enough, but if you need two, join with a French seam, 20cm (8in) checked ribbon for each eyelet
Pole: Metal pole bent to fit your shower area and mounted at least 30cm (12in) above the shower head with 5 – 6 curtain rings per metre (yard), 1.5cm (¾in) eyelet set with the same number of eyelets as rings plus three eyelets for each side

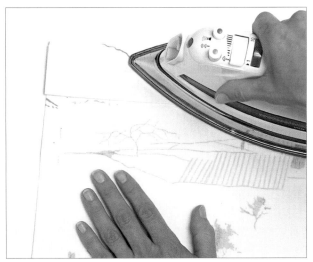

1 Press 4cm (1⅝in) to the wrong side along both sides of your fabric. Press in half to make a 2cm (¾in) double hem. Pin, tack and machine stitch close to the folded edge. Press 10cm (4in) to the wrong side at the top and bottom of the fabric. Press in half to make a 5cm (2in) double hem. Pin, tack then machine stitch close to the folded edge and again 0.5cm (½in) from the outer edge. Press.

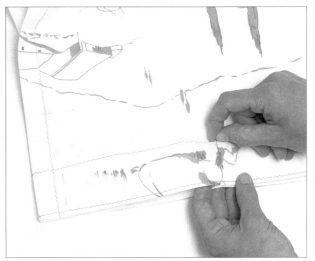

2 Make the same turnings on the under curtain – if you have bought a shower curtain you won't need to do anything to it. Place the waterproof curtain flat onto your worktable, right side down with the outer curtain on top right side up, pin together. They should be almost exactly the same size, but don't worry if they are not – ease the spare fullness evenly across the width.

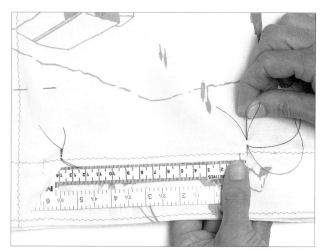

3 Mark the eyelet positions of both curtains with tacks; make the first two 5cm (2in) from each end, divide the remaining width into approximately 20cm (8in) gaps. Also mark three positions down each side, with 40cm (16in) between each, the last eyelet should be at least 100cm (40in) from the hem – the waterproof curtain can then be lifted inside the shower while the outer curtain remains outside.

4 Make the holes and punch the eyelets through, following the instructions with the eyelet kit. Using lengths of ribbon, tie the curtains together through each pair of holes and knot. Tie the ribbons to the top eyelets through the curtain pole rings. If you find that you need to weight the inner curtain a little, punch eyelets through this layer only, at the two bottom corners.

TUCKED CURTAINS

A curtain in linen scrim will absorb up to 20% of its weight in water, and can be machine washed and dried. This pin tucked curtain is very feminine and light, or use layers of muslin for an ethereal, romantic, effect.

Drawstring bags

Draw string bags couldn't be simpler to make and perform a myriad of functions in the home. Make over-sized bags in white cotton, mattress ticking or towelling for great laundry bags. Use muslin for tiny lavender bags to hang in the wardrobe, or a floral print filled with herbs for the airing cupboard or laundry room. Use any hard wearing fabric to hold gym kits, shoes or toys.

A whole series of drawstring bags in different shapes, sizes and fabrics are invaluable for travelling. Separate bags keep items in shape, and protect everything from walking shoes, toiletries and soft knitwear to a carefully rolled taffeta evening gown.

MATERIALS:

Choose a non-fray fabric strong enough for the use of the bag – towelling or strong cotton, shower proof fabric if the bag is intended to hold damp items, matching sewing thread

FABRIC:

Laundry bag: For a bag 50cm (20in) wide x 72cm (28in) high you will need one piece of strong cotton fabric 160cm (1¾yd) x 55cm (22in), shower curtain lining fabric same size as the main fabric – this is optional, if you are using lining first baste it to the main fabric and use as one, 3m (3⅓yd) cotton or linen cord 6mm (¼in) diameter
For other bags: You will need fabric 42cm (16½in) x 15cm (6in) wide for a lavender bag and 90cm (36in) x 35cm (14in) for a shoe bag

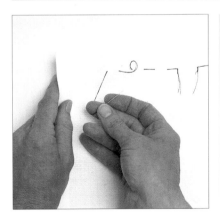

1 Fold the fabric in half widthways, right sides together so that the short ends meet. Taking a 1.5cm (½in) seam allowance, pin, tack and machine stitch each side from the folded edge to within 18cm (7in) of the raw edges. Leave a gap of 2cm (¾in), stitch to the end.

2 Neaten the seams with pinking shears, then press flat. Turn over the top raw edge of the bag 1.5cm (½in), pin and tack the turn. Fold the top edge over again so that the tacked fold line finishes just below the holes left in the side seams. Pin and tack.

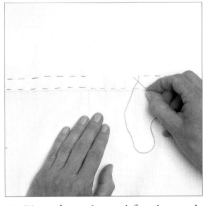

3 To make a channel for the cord, hand or machine stitch all around the top of the bag, 0.5cm (¼in) from the folded edge. Make a second row of stitching 2cm (¾in) above the first. Before threading the cord through the channel, decorate with embroidery or appliqué shapes.

4 Press the bag. Attach a bodkin needle or safety pin to the end of the cord. Thread the cord through the stitched channel, leaving a loop at both side openings or thread the cord through the fabric channel. Test for length, then cut and knot the cord ends securely together.

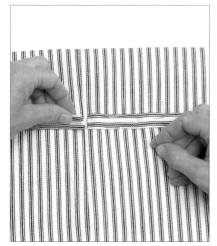

5 Another way to make the channel is to add a strip of fabric to the outside surface of the bag. Cut a length of fabric to fit around the bag, 4cm (1⅝in) wide. Press under both long edges then stitch the band to the finished bag. Start and finish on a side seam and leave the join open for the cord.

Towels

It is possible to buy good cotton terry towelling, flat weave linens and cottons by the metre to make your own towels, or you could decorate good quality plain ready made towels bought cheaply at sale time. Bind the edges of the towels with fabric, in a colour to co-ordinate with your room decoration. Off-cuts of fabric can be employed for appliqué and bindings and if you enjoy hand embroidery, add initials or a decorative edge to the towels and flannels.

MATERIALS:

Looped cotton, linen or flat waffle weave – towels will be frequently washed and often at high temperatures, so the fabrics and ribbon should be washed at 90 degrees to check they are colourfast and to take out any possible shrinkage, washable fabric with motif for appliqué, iron-on stiffening, ribbon or fabric off-cuts for edge binding, embroidery thread, matching sewing thread

FABRIC:

Small Towel: For a finished size of 50cm x 70cm (20in x 28in) you will need 53cm x 100cm (21in x 39½in) of fabric
Large Towel: For a finished size of 50 x 90cm (20in x 35½in) you will need 53cm x 120cm (21in x 47¼in) of fabric
Allow a 1.5cm (⅝in) turning on each long side and 15cm (6in) on the short edges

EMBROIDERED EDGINGS

1 To finish the edges of the towel without binding, make a double turn on the edges of the fabric, with a larger turn on one short edge. Pin and tack the seams. Remove the pins, press flat.

2 Using embroidery thread, work a row of large evenly spaced running stitches close to the inner folded edge. Make another row just above the first, lining the stitches up with the gaps in the first.

3 Using a contrasting coloured thread, weave in and out of the two parallel rows of stitches making a decorative zig-zag stitch. The same thread can be used to embroider initials onto the towel.

BINDING

Either ribbon or off-cuts of fabric can be used to wrap over the ends of the towel. This should look the same from both sides. For a 4cm (1⅝in) binding cut strips of fabric the width of the towel plus 3cm (1¼in) for the ends x 12cm (5in) wide. Press under 1.5cm (⅝in) along each long edge and 1.5cm (⅝in) at the ends. Fold the binding over the towel end, pin in place and tack through to hold both sides firmly. Stitch close to the folded edge – you will need to make sure that the folded edges are exactly above each other so that as you stitch, you sew through both sides equally.

BORDER EDGING

Use either ribbons or fabric off-cuts to edge the end of the towel. If using fabric, cut strips the width of your towel plus 3cm (1¼in) for the ends and 2cm (¾in) wider than you want the finished edging to be. Press under 1cm (½in) along each long side and 1.5cm (⅝in) at each end. Pin and tack to the towel. Stitch with tight zigzag stitches over the edge or straight stitch just inside the folded edge. Ribbon can just be pinned and tacked on with the ends folded under to neaten and stitched in the same way.

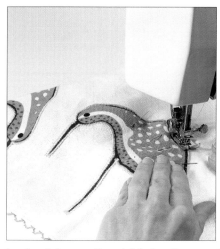

APPLIQUÉ

Appliqué is the needlework term for stitching one cut-out piece of fabric onto another larger piece. The cut-out might be a felt star cut freehand or a design from a printed fabric which is contained enough to be able to cut neatly around. The cut-out should be in proportion to the finished article.

To prevent fraying, iron a lightweight stiffening onto the back of the appliqué fabric. Cut neatly around the shape. Pin and tack the shape securely onto the towel using small stitches. Set the machine to a tight zigzag and stitch around the outer edge of the shape. Always experiment on a spare piece of fabric before embarking on the real project. Remove the tacking stitches and press.

Storage boxes

We all need storage boxes, and often make do with old shoe boxes, shirt boxes or chocolate boxes left over from other purchases. These are usually quite sturdy and suitable for covering with fabric, so with a little time you could make the storage cupboard or wardrobe much more interesting. Use different fabric to colour code the contents, even fabrics printed with a themed design. For the office, cover boxes to store disks, videos, CDs, all manner of papers, photographs and birthday cards. Larger boxes are good for storing out of season clothes and linens. You can buy plain card boxes from department stores which are inexpensive and sturdy enough to take a fabric covering.

MATERIALS:

Any medium weight, tightly woven cotton poplin or chintz, plain or patterned, brushed, twill or any flat weave. Patterned fabrics will hide any discrepancies if the box is a bit bent and has less than perfect corners or joins. For the lining use a non-fraying fabric, felt, paper backed fabric or paper, PVA water soluble glue; 2.5cm (1in) brush

FABRIC:

Main Fabric: For a shoe box 30cm x 15cm x 8cm (12in x 6in x 3in) high, you will need, one piece 92cm x 12cm (37in x 4in) for the box sides, one piece 28cm x 43cm (11in x 17in) for the outer lid

Box Lining: Non-fray lining fabric – inner base 30cm x 15cm (12in x 6in), inner lid 30cm x 15cm (12in x 6in), outer base 29cm x 14cm (11½in x 5½in), two inner sides 32cm x 8cm (13in x 3in), two inner ends 15cm x 8cm (6in x 3in)

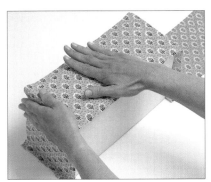

1 Add a little cold water to the glue to make it easier to work. Apply glue to one box end and one side. Place the long length of fabric on the table. Position the box end on the fabric leaving 1.5cm (⅝in) all around. Roll the box onto the pasted sides. Press the fabric flat to remove any bubbles.

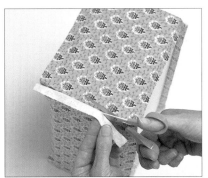

2 At the first corner, stick the 1.5cm (⅝in) overlap from the end to the long side. Glue the second end and side. Roll the box to attach the remaining fabric. To neaten the last corner, trim the fabric along the side of the box with sharp scissors. The cut should be neat and the corners invisible.

3 Glue 1.5cm (⅝in) along the base of the box and press the fabric flap onto the glue. At the top of the box overlap the corners if the fabric is lightweight, or for heavier fabric cut away a triangle at each corner. Glue 1.5cm (⅝in) inside the box, turn over the fabric flap and press onto the glue.

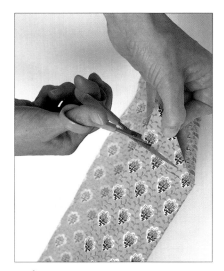

4 Paste the box lid and place centrally onto the lid fabric, turn over and smooth flat. Glue the two ends then press the fabric flap onto the glue. Pin the fabric tight to the corners. Fold then trim back to 1cm (½in) from the corner. Remove the pins and paste the flaps onto the sides.

5 Paste the inner ends of the lid and 1cm (½in) onto each side. Fold the fabric flap over, using the scissors to push it into the corners. Repeat for the inner sides. At the corners fold under the 1cm (½in) flaps. Snip away the fold from the bottom of the lid then fold one layer back inside the lid.

6 To line inside the box, apply glue to the long sides and 1cm (½in) onto both the short ends and the base. Press in the side fabric, starting 0.5cm (¼in) from the top so the lining extends onto the base. Score the creases. Glue in the ends, inner and outer base and the inner lid.

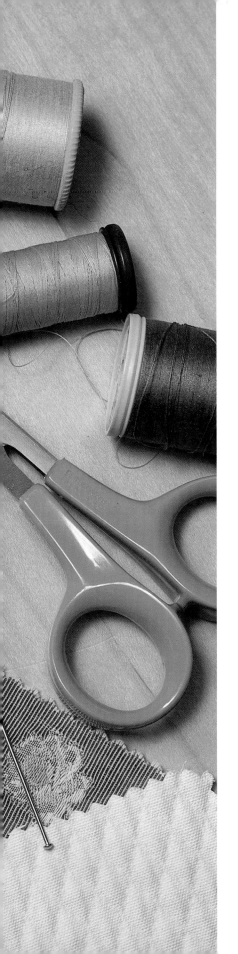

Tools and Techniques

This chapter covers the tools and techniques needed to create soft furnishing projects for the bedroom and bathroom.

Choosing the correct tool for the job is as important as the right colour or weight of fabric. Most of the tools used in these projects you will find in a standard sewing kit. To get the best results buy the very best equipment you can afford; good cutting scissors; sharp needles and pins and a strong measuring tape.

As we all have different sized beds, duvets and pillows, a section on measuring gives you all the information needed to correctly estimate the amount of fabric for each of the soft furnishing projects in the book.

Good care and regular cleaning will keep your furnishings in good condition. At the end of this chapter you will find a section giving useful information to help protect and value your efforts.

Essential sewing kit

Good quality tools last and make it easier to achieve consistently good results, so choose the best you can afford. A sewing box with compartments is a very useful addition to your sewing kit, keeping everything separate and easy to find.

MEASURING AND MARKING

Tape measure: a vital part of any sewing kit. Choose a tape measure made of nylon or some other material that will not stretch and has metal protective ends. Each side of the tape should start and finish at opposite ends so that you do not have to unwind the tape to find the starting point.

Steel tape: the most reliable tool for measuring items like beds, windows and curtains when working out quantities of material required.

Metre or yard stick: important for measuring lengths of fabric and for marking straight lines. Make sure that it is straight, has not warped and that the markings appear on both sides.

Tailor's chalk: comes in a range of colours but white is easiest to remove later. Keep the edge sharp or alternatively use a dressmaker's pencil which has a brush for removing the marks.

Pencil: for copying patterns onto tracing paper. A soft pencil such as a 2B, is the easiest to use.

CUTTING

Pinking shears: have serrated blades which make a zig zag cut. They are used to neaten raw edges, particularly on fabrics that fray easily.

Cutting-out scissors: should have a 15cm (6in) blade and be flat on one side. Never use on any other material except fabric.

Needlework scissors: are necessary for snipping threads, cutting into or notching seams and other close trimming jobs.

Paper scissors: are needed for cutting paper templates and patterns. Never use to cut fabric, or thread.

STITCHING

Pins: come in a wide range of sizes. Those with glass or plastic heads are the most visible and easiest to use. Use a pin cushion to store pins when working.

Sewing needles: keep an assortment of needles in your sewing kit. The most useful sizes range from 3-10. The higher the number the finer the needle. Betweens, are short sharp needles that are ideal for fine hemming. Sharps, which are longer and allow more than one stitch on the needle at a time, are useful for tacking or gathering. There is also a wide range of specialist needles available, including a tapestry needle, which has an eye large enough to take narrow ribbon.

Thimble: protects your fingertip when hand sewing.

Threads: mercerised cotton is ideal for stitching cotton or linen; buy silk thread for silk fabric; thread with a coating of cotton for synthetic fabrics; cotton thread for wool; a polyester/cotton mix for man-made fibres and for stretchy fabrics use a polyester thread. Choose 36 for general use, 50 or 60 for finer fabrics.

Needle threader: the flexible wire loop is pushed through the needle's eye, the thread is then inserted into the loop and the loop and thread pulled back through the eye of the needle.

MACHINE WORK

Sewing machine: essential for joining seams and any hems. A sewing machine that does straight stitch, zig zag and can reverse is all you need to make the projects in this book.

Machine needles: are available in a range of sizes. Choose fine needles and fine threads when working with fine fabrics; thicker needles and thicker threads on heavier fabrics.

Machine feet: come in a range of designs for specific jobs. Apart from a standard foot you will find a one-sized zipper or piping foot, which can be adjusted to the right or left, a very useful asset. A roller foot works well on shiny fabrics, and a transparent foot will help with applique work – you can see the fabric more easily. Before you use a different foot on any sewing project, practise some stitching on a scrap piece of fabric – that way you can be sure of the results.

Measuring and estimating

Soft furnishing projects need to be tailored to fit the house style, room size or colour, window or bed for which they are intended. By following these instructions and the measurements given within the projects you will be able to make covers, curtains and bedding that will fit well and look better than you ever thought was possible to make at home.

BED VALANCE

Measure the bare bed frame to work out the fabric requirements for making a valance. Whatever style of bed you have, the skirt needs to fall around the corners without interruption. Cut the base fabric roughly to size – this is called the platform. Lay this over the bed, draw around any posts and shaped corners, allowing 2cm (¾in) for seams, you may want to edge the platform with strips of the skirt fabric. The valance skirt can be made as one or split around corner posts: it can be pleated or gathered along the length or corners. Measure the skirt adding a 6cm (2½in) hem allowance and 2cm (¾in) to the top and sides. Allow two and a half times around the bed for gathers. The 'pleats' at each corner are neater made as separate flaps: each flap should be 45 - 50cm (18 - 20in) wide.

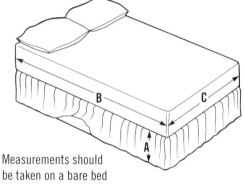

Measurements should be taken on a bare bed
A: Mattress/base length
B: Mattress/base width
C: Skirt length – top of base to floor

BEDCOVER

Take measurements over both summer and winter bedding to get the exact finished size. Generally you will need to allow an extra 3cm (1¼in) on the bed height for summer bedding and 5cm (2in) for winter.
Standard bedcovers are 250cm x 200cm (100in x 80in) – this makes a floor length cover for a single bed or a valance length cover for a small double 135cm x 190cm (54in x 75in).

A cover 250cm (100in) square will make a floor length cover for a standard double bed 150cm x 190cm (60in x 75in) and a top cover for a king sized bed 180cm x 190cm (72in x 75in).

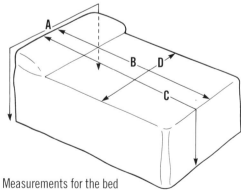

Measurements for the bed cover should be taken over your usual bedding
A: Twice the height of the bed over the pillows, plus the width
B: Top to the bottom of the bed
C: Top to the bottom, plus height at the bottom
D: Width of the bed

PILLOW

Pillows come in two shapes – the traditional pillow shape which is approximately 50cm x 75cm (20in x 30in) and the continental which is either 65cm (26in), 70cm (28in) or 75cm (30in) square. Always measure your pads before making the covers as they can vary from country to country. When making covers allow at least 1.5cm (⅝in) in each direction, plus the seam allowances.

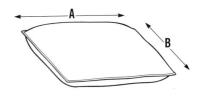

A: Length   **B: Width**

BED FRAME

Four posters and half testers need one curtain to fit behind the bed head and either four bed curtains or two side curtains for the corners.

If you are re-furbishing an existing frame you will be able to follow the original fittings to find the sizes. The amount of fullness you should allow will depend on the period of the bed. A substantial bed should have curtains which are heavy but not over full whereas a light, metal frame will take up to four times fullness of fine fabrics.

If building your own frame, allow enough depth on the wood to include fittings for curtains, ceiling drape and outer pelmet. The frame should be approximately 15cm (6in) larger all around than the bed to allow adequate space for bedding and curtains.

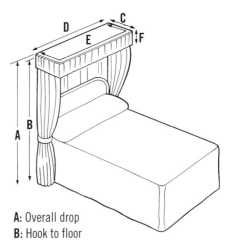

A: Overall drop
B: Hook to floor
C: Width of side curtains
D: Pelmet back curtain
E: Pelmet length, plus twice the width.
F: Pelmet drop

DUVET

Try to find wide width fabric, but if that is not possible and you want the duvet to match another fabric in the room, use a bought sheet for the under side with your furnishing fabric on the top. Always leave the centre panel as a whole width of fabric with joins at either side: cover the joins with an interesting tape, or insert piping.

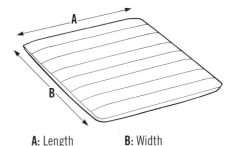

A: Length   **B: Width**

YOUR WORKTABLE

A good work surface can save you a considerable amount of time and stress. Even if you are going to make just one item it is worth spending a little time to give yourself the best surface to work on. A dining room or kitchen table will be quite adequate for smaller items and the floor for larger ones. But the surface must be smooth, flat and grease free. You should be able to pin into the surface and to iron over it. It also helps if your work can remain undisturbed throughout the project.

For an 'instant' worktable, cover a piece of sturdy MDF board: use an old blanket or curtain interlining, with a piece of canvas or curtain lining over. Pull tight and staple the cloth to the underside. Buy the biggest board that you can accommodate – for most projects 2.4m x 1.2m x 2cm thick (8ft x 4ft x ¾in) is ideal. Rest it on a table, a guest bed, or on the floor. Afterwards store the board in the garage for later use.

Seams

Making your stitching look as neat on the wrong side as it does on the right, not only looks more professional but also helps to ensure a long lasting finish. There are several ways to secure raw edges and the most suitable techniques will depend on the weight and type of fabric used.

PRESSING SEAMS

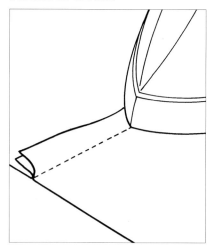

1 Press each seam as soon as you have sewn it. Work on the wrong side, following the line of stitches. Hold the iron over one area, before lifting it and transferring it to the next.

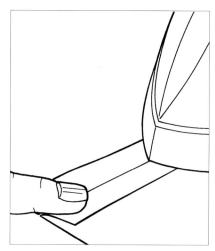

2 Slide your fingers down the seam to open it, then with the point of the iron press the seamline open. Finally, press down the allowance at either side using the full base of the iron.

PRESSING DELICATE FABRICS

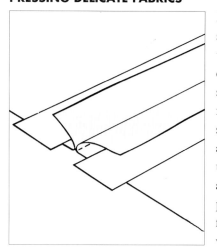

If pressing a seam is likely to leave marks on the right side of the fabric, cut thin strips of card and slip these under the seam allowance to protect the fabric. Fabric with a deep pile like velvet is easily crushed. Press using steam and a minimum of pressure, wrong side up, with a spare piece of fabric, pile side up, underneath.

NEATENING SEAMS

To avoid raw edges fraying, it is best to neaten the edges of all seam allowances. There are several ways to secure raw edges and the most suitable technique will depend on the weight and type of fabric used.

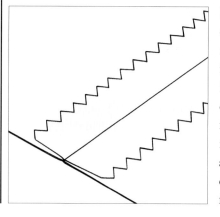

Pinking: this quick and easy method of finishing seams is suitable for cotton and fine fabrics that do not fray. Test on a scrap before cutting the finished seam.

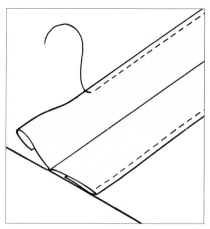

Straight stitch folded edge: this method is ideal for light to medium-weight fabrics that are not bulky. Turn under a seam allowance of 5mm (¼in), press then straight stitch the edge to hold it in place.

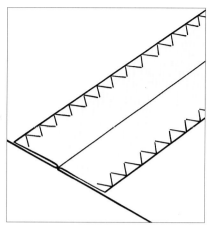

Zig zag edging: this is the most commonly used method for neatening raw edges and is good for bulky fabric or those that fray. Stitch using a short, narrow zig zag, trim just short of the stitches: on fabrics that fray badly use a wider stitch.

FLAT SEAM

The raw edges of a flat seam are encased within the seam line but, unlike a French seam, both lines of stitching appear on the surface of the fabric.

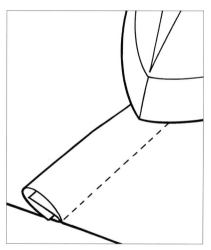

1 With right sides together, machine stitch 1.5cm (⅜in) inside the raw edges. Press the seam allowance to one side. Trim the underside of the seam allowance to 5mm (¼in).

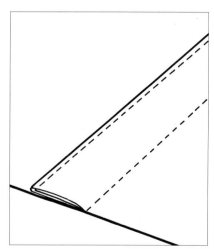

2 Press the wider seam allowance in half with the narrower allowance encased within. Press then pin the seam flat on the fabric. Tack then machine stitch close to the folded edge.

FRENCH SEAMS

This seam encloses the raw edges of fabric, and is used when an untidy edge might be visible. With the wrong sides of fabric together, stitch approximately 6mm (¼in) from the raw edges. Refold with right sides together, pin and stitch again just beyond the first stitching line, to enclose the raw edges within the seam. When stitching heavier fabrics, allow 1cm (⅜in) for the first stitching line.

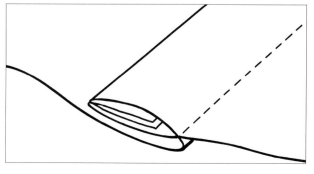

Hand stitches

Hand sewing is necessary for specific stages of the making-up process and is essential for creating a professional looking finish. The stitches illustrated here are used in the making-up of the projects in this book.

SLIPSTITCHING HEMS

Slipstitching creates a neat finish for all hems as the stitches are almost invisible on the right side of the fabric.

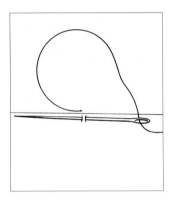

1 Fasten the thread with a backstitch within the fabric of the hem and then bring the needle out on the folded edge of the hem. Pick up one thread, or at the most two, from the main fabric, close to the hem.

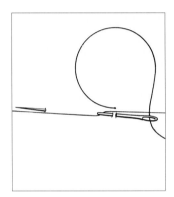

2 Take a stitch of 1-2cm (⅜ - ¾in) along the fold of the hem and pull the thread through. Continue picking up threads from the main fabric and taking stitches along the hem edge until the hem is stitched.

LADDER STITCH

This is used to join two folded edges together and to close a gap left in the stitching when turning fabric through to the right side.

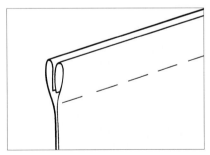

1 Fold under a narrow hem on both pieces of fabric to be joined. Tack loosely to hold the folded edges together. Make a small stitch to fasten the thread within the fold.

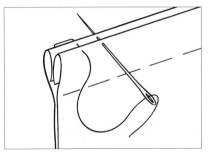

2 Bring the thread out on the outer side of one fold. Make a small stitch along the fold, push the needle through the fabric bringing it out exactly on the opposite fold.

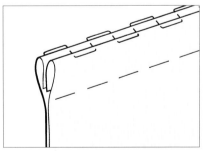

3 Continue until the opening is closed. Do not pull the thread too tight and if possible make the stitches and thread invisible. The stitches should be 1.5cm (½in) in length.

LOCKSTITCH

Used to join two layers of fabric together so they act as one. Lockstitch is worked vertically to join the seams and then once or twice more between each seam.

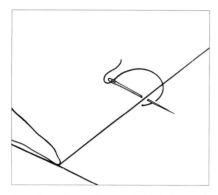

1 Lay fabric together with wrong sides facing. Pin on the centre line, vertically down the length of the fabric. Fold back the lining to the pinned line.

Starting about 30cm (12in) from the lower edge secure the thread in the lining with a knot. Make a tiny stitch in the main fabric, picking up just one thread. Leave a 2.5cm (1in) gap, then make a one-thread stitch from the lining back to the top fabric, working over the thread to form a simple loop.

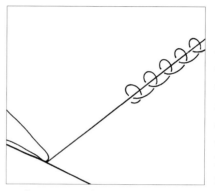

2 Continue making locking stitches every 2.5cm (1in) until you reach the top edge – keep the thread very loose to stop the fabric from puckering. Unfold the fabric before smoothing the layers back together. Make another vertical row of pins 38cm (15in) from the last. Fold back the lining, continue making rows of stitches across the complete width of the fabric until the layers are joined and they act as one.

PATTERN MATCHING

This is the professional method used to tack two pieces of patterned fabric together, working on the right side of the fabric, so that the pattern matches across the seam. It can be used as a permanent seam if you make smaller stitches.

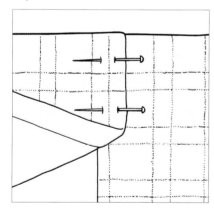

1 On one of the two pieces of fabric to be joined, press under 1.25cm (½in) along the edge. Then place this folded edge, with raw edges matching, over the second piece of fabric. Match the pattern and pin in position.

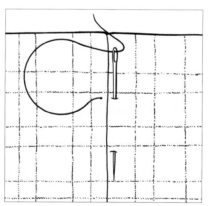

2 Secure the thread, with small stitches, within the fold line. Make a small stitch across to the flat fabric and running directly down the side of the fold, bring the needle out 1.5-2cm (½-¾in) further down the seamline.

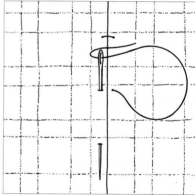

3 Take the needle straight across the fold and push it down inside the folded edge for another 1.5-2cm (½-¾in). Repeat these two stitches for the length of the seam. Turn the fabric to the wrong side to finish the seam.

FRENCH KNOT

These small surface knots are used to add detail to embroidered curtains and bedding.

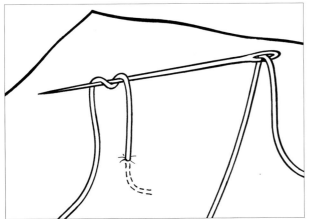 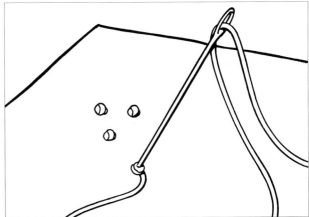

1 Push the needle up through the fabric where you want to make the first knot. Pull the thread taut with one hand while twisting the needle around the thread several times.

2 Push the needle back through the fabric at the point where it emerged, leaving a knot on the surface of the fabric. Fasten off the thread or go on to the next stitch.

SATIN STITCH

Satin stitch can be done on any swing needle sewing machine or by hand.

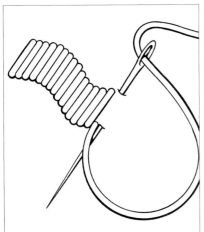 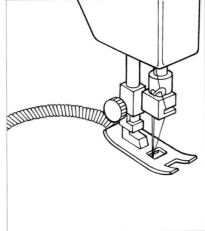

By hand: if the stitching area will not fit under your machine foot or you prefer to embroider by hand, using an embroidery needle and thread make long, straight stitches close together, keeping the thread flat and even.

Machine: set the zig zag button so that the stitches are wide and close together. It may appear as a buttonhole stitch on your machine. Always test the stitch on a spare piece of fabric for length of stitch and spacing.

CROSS STITCH

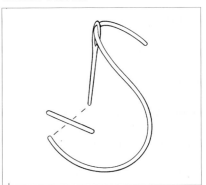

The simplicity of basic cross stitch makes it a highly popular stitch. When used on soft furnishings, stitches are usually worked in rows of even slanted stitches across the fabric, first from right to left laying down half the crosses, then back from left to right to complete them. When the stitches are to be seen from both sides of the fabric, care should be taken to ensure the back of your work is as neat as the front.

GATHERING

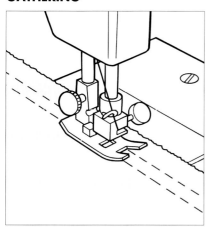

1 Set your machine using the stitch length regulator to the longest straight stitch. It is best to run two lines of stitching next to each other about 5mm (¼in) apart.

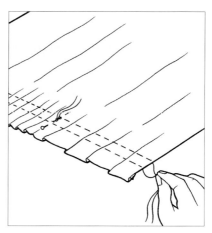

2 Pull up the two lines of threads checking that the gathers are even along the fabric. Work in 60cm (24in) sections. Secure the pulled threads around a pin to hold before stitching.

HERRINGBONE STITCH

This is the stitch used to fix a raw edged hem in position prior to covering it with a lining, or to attach curtain interlining.

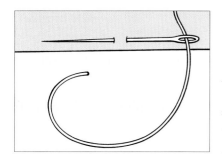

1 Tack the hem or interlining in place. Secure the thread with a few stitches, then bring the needle up through it, working from left to right. Take the thread diagonally to the main fabric and make a small backstitch picking up one to two threads.

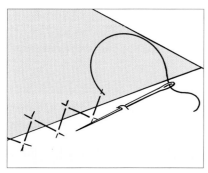

2 Still working diagonally, move across to the hem or interlining and make another small backstitch through this layer only. Continue in this way making stitches on both fabrics to the end of the seam before securing the thread.

BLANKET AND BUTTONHOLE STITCH

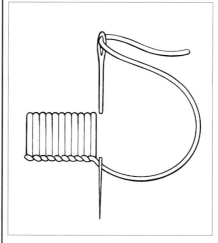

This stitch is used not only to make buttonholes but in any situation which requires strength: this scroll-like stitch is worked close together forming a firm edge which will resist abrasion when rubbed against metal poppers, hooks and eyes and brass rings. When worked further apart, this stitch now called Blanket, can be used to cover a raw edge or worked over a folded edge. Make the stitches of equal length and along parallel lines. Working from left to right, push the needle up through the fabric on the lower line, insert it a short distance away on the upper line, working back towards the lower. Bring the needle out close to where it first emerged, looping the thread under the needle. Pull up the thread tightening the stitch, to form a scroll-like base on the edge of the fabric. Continue making stitches in this way along the edge of the fabric, or around the buttonhole.

Closures

Openings can be unobtrusive like zips, or obvious and used as part of the design. Brightly coloured buttons or pretty ribbon loops or ties make the opening a feature, adding an extra dimension to the finished design.

FOLDED TIES

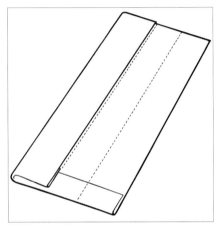

1 Cut a strip of fabric four times the width of your finished tie and 3cm (1⅛in) longer. Turn over one short end, 1cm (¼ in). Press in half lengthways.

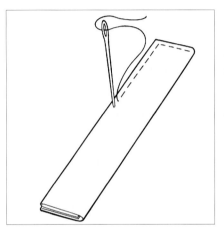

2 With wrong sides together, fold each side to the middle, press. Fold over again and stitch the short and long side together close to the folded edge.

ROULEAU TIES

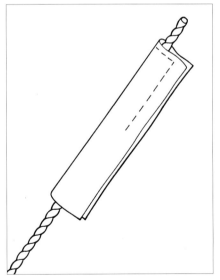

1 Cut a strip of fabric four times the width of your finished tie and 3cm (1⅛in) longer. Fold in half lengthways, right sides together, enclosing a length of cord or string. Stitch across the short side to hold the cord and down the length, halfway across the width.

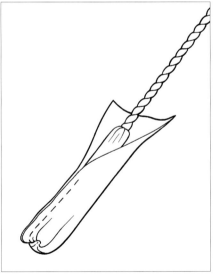

2 Trim back the fabric raw edges to 2.5mm (⅛in), and across the stitched corner to reduce the bulk. Pull the cord gently from the free end, while at the same time turning the rouleau right side out. Cut off the cord and neaten the ends with small neat slip stitches.

PLACKET CLOSURE WITH TIES

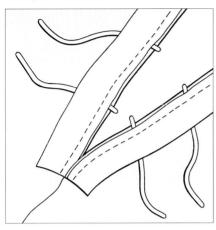

1 Cut two lengths of fabric each 12cm (5in) wide and 4cm (1⅝in) longer than the opening. Mark the tie positions on both sides of the opening, pin in place. Pin one of the plackets to each side of the opening, right sides together, over the ties.

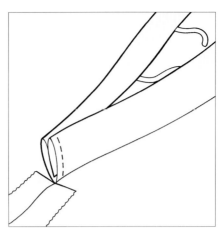

2 Stitch along the seam allowances. Press each strip into three, enclosing the raw edges. Slip stitch, using small neat stitches, along the length of both strips to hold them in place. Pin the short, raw ends of the plackets together. Stitch to hold them in place.

PLACKET CLOSURE WITH BUTTONS AND ROULEAU

A rouleau of ribbon can be inserted into the placket to loop over each button. Gauge the ribbon length to suit the button size. The loops are attached to the right side of the fabric, with the loop ends enclosed within the placket pieces.

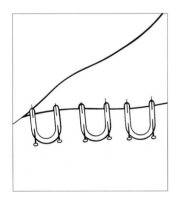

1 Cut two lengths of fabric each 12cm (5in) wide and 4cm (1⅝in) longer than the opening. Mark the button positions. Cut short lengths of ribbon which are then pinned in loops to one side of the opening.

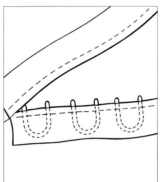

2 On the right side of the fabric and with right sides together, pin the placket strips down the sides of the opening, securing the rouleau loops onto the fabric. Stitch along the seam allowance. Press.

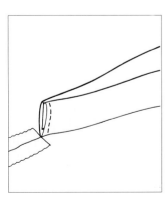

3 Fold each strip into three to enclose the raw edges, slip stitch along the length of both strips to hold them in place. Pin the short, raw edges of the placket strips together. Stitch to hold them in place.

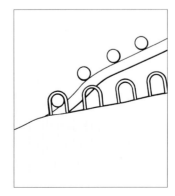

4 Stitch a button onto the placket edge to correspond with each loop. Press carefully on both sides. Before stitching the ribbon loops in position, check that they will fit snugly over the buttons.

Piping

Piping fabric can be cut either on the straight or on the cross; if the piping is used in straight lines then it will be easier to handle cut straight; if it is to be bent around corners then it should be cut on the cross. For making piping, cut 4cm (1½in) wide fabric strips or slightly wider 5.5cm (2⅛in) for loose covers. All joins should be made on the cross to minimise bulk and the ends cut across at 90 degrees.

CUTTING THE PIPING FABRIC

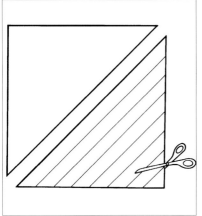

1 With the fabric flat on the table fold one bottom corner up, making half of a 30cm (12in) square. Cut along the fold line. Pencil lines the width of the strip, following the cut line across the fabric. Cut along these lines, repeat for the other half of the fabric.

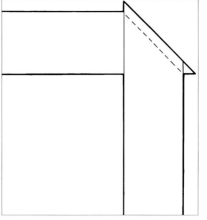

2 Hold two strips of fabric together as if making a continuous strip of piping. Turn the top strip over so that it is at a 45 degree angle to the first. With right sides, raw edges together, pin, tack then stitch along the seamline.

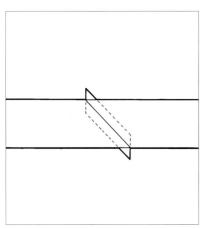

3 Join enough lengths of fabric until you have a continuous strip, long enough to fit around the edge of the article you are making. Open out the seams, trim away the extra triangles of fabric on the seam allowance. Press seams flat from the right side of the fabric.

MAKING THE PIPING

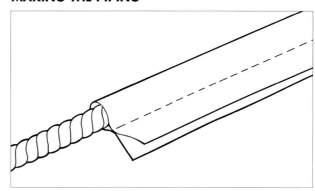

Fold the length of piping fabric in half lengthways. Insert the piping cord. With raw edges together machine stitch along the length encasing the cord.

JOINING PIPING

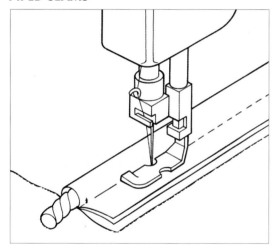

To join the piping ends, after you have attached the piping and stitched nearly to the starting position, cut the piping off leaving an overlap of 6cm (2⅜in). Unpick the casing and cut away the cord so that the two ends butt together. Fold the piping fabric across at a 45 degree angle and cut along this fold. Turn under 1cm (⅜in) and pin securely before stitching to complete the piped edge.

PIPED SEAMS

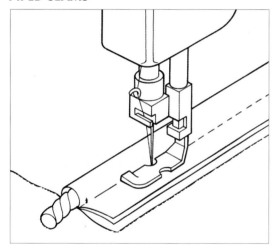

1 Always attach the piping so that the raw edges of the piping line up exactly with the raw edges of the main fabric. The seam allowance is usually 1.5cm (⅝in). Pin along the stitching line and also at right angles, especially near the corners. These right angled pins can be left in whilst machining and will keep the piping flat. Using a piping foot on the machine, stitch down the seamline.

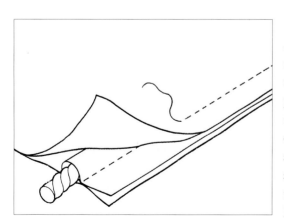

2 Place the second fabric piece over the first, right sides together, encasing the piping cord and matching the raw edges. Pin, tack and stitch down the seamline again, using the previous stitching line as a guide.

CURVED SEAMS

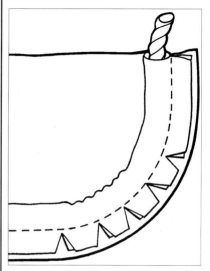

The piping cord should be snipped at 1-2cm (⅜-¾in) intervals to stay flat around a convex curve. Notches will need to be cut away at similar intervals for a concave curve.

SHARP CORNERS

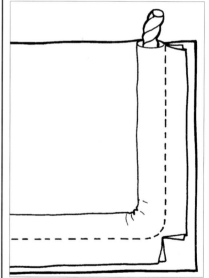

At each corner stop 1.5cm (⅝in) from the turn and snip right into the piping stitching line. Fold the piping sharply and pin to make a square corner.

Fabric care

Having spent many hours making your own soft furnishings, spend a little time learning to care for them. Careful cleaning and pressing will pay off. The result will not just be more attractive, but also give your precious fabrics a longer life.

EVERYDAY CARE

Dust, cigarette smoke, solid fuel or gas fires are the main threats to soft furnishings, along with accidental spills and staining. Regular vacuuming will help to extend the life of fabric – removing particles of dust or smoke before they become embedded. Furnishings should be vacuumed regularly with a soft brush attachment. Vacuum in line with the fabric, not against the grain.

Great care should be taken with stains: the use of stain removal products should be treated with caution, spot treatments can easily end up as permanent marks. It is advisable to choose washable fabrics for furnishings especially if they are to be in constant use.

Modern printed or dyed fabric has good resistance to fading, though all fabric does eventually fade. It is a good idea to protect fabric, wherever possible, from long exposure to direct sunlight. This applies especially where only part of the fabric is prone to exposure, fading will of course show much more when it is next to an area protected from the sun. For this reason it is best to always line curtains and draw them back during the day.

Make sure that curtains and blinds do not hang too close to windows or radiators: condensation and excessive heat can have detrimental effects, especially in combination.

WASHING AND CLEANING

Wash items before they become badly soiled and treat stains immediately. The water temperature is an important consideration. In order to avoid shrinkage and colour fading it is advisable to wash bed linen at no more than 60 degrees centigrade.

Always follow the manufacturer's instructions regarding the recommended cleaning procedures, if you have bought pre-made items, this will be indicated by the standard set of symbols, which are also found in clothing. Where dry cleaning is advised there may still be some minimal shrinkage due to the process used. Some fabrics such as chintz need to be dry cleaned in a non-water charged system. Check that your dry cleaner is knowledgeable. If shrinkage has occurred it may be possible, in some cases, to iron the damp fabric in the direction of the shrinkage whilst gently stretching it. Always test the fabric for shrinkage before making up furnishings for bathroom use.

If you are unsure if a fabric is colourfast, check it before washing with other items. Dip a small, hidden area in warm water, then place this damp area between two white cloths and iron until the fabric is dry. If there is any colour on the cloths, the fabric is not colourfast and the item should be washed separately. Never use bleach when washing soft furnishings. Be aware that most washing powders contain some bleaching or brightening enzymes. It may be advisable to use a mild liquid detergent to avoid colours fading.

DRYING AND PRESSING

Do not dry fabric too quickly as this could result in shrinkage and creasing, this is especially important if tumble drying. When ironing, care should be taken to set the iron at the correct temperature. Iron whilst still damp for best results. Iron chintz fabrics on the face side with a dry iron, and the steam off.

Press any embroidery on the wrong side, on a soft towel to avoid flattening the stitching. Take care with rayon thread and any metallic or glittery yarn, the iron could easily melt your stitchery. Do not press lace, just lay out flat and pin in position, leaving until dry.

STAIN REMOVAL

- When removing a stain, never scrub it: work from the edges, dabbing at the stain until it disappears. Scrubbing spreads the damage.

- On liquid stains, including wine, cover the area with salt to draw up as much liquid as possible. Then place the item in cold water to soak for half to one hour. Finish by washing in the usual way.

- Tea and coffee stains should be soaked immediately in pre-wash biological powder, then washed in the usual way.

- On fruit and fruit juice stains, rub fabric with salt before soaking in cold water. Rub with neat liquid detergent. Finish by washing in the usual way.

- On biological stains, such as blood or milk, soak fabric in biological detergent before washing.

- With solids, scrape off as much as you can with a flat knife before treating the stain.

WHAT CAN GO WRONG?

Shrinkage is the main problem caused by improper cleaning. All woven fabrics do tend to shrink, especially those made of natural fibres – like cotton. It is normal for furnishing fabrics to shrink by around 5% when washed. Dry cleaning too can cause shrinkage, but to a lesser degree. It is sensible to make curtains with a generous hem, and leave them loosely tacked until the first clean. Common sense is the message for avoiding frightening results: avoid bleaches of any sort, including washing liquids and powders with added bleach. Don't dry fabrics too quickly or with too much heat. Iron while still damp with the iron at the right temperature. Above all, if you have the washing instructions, follow them carefully.

CUSHION CARE

- Shake out and air pads regularly. Hang the cushions outside in a cotton bag on warm days to freshen the fabrics and feather filling.

- When washing covers, close zips and fastenings.

- Wash feather pads in warm soapy water and rinse well. Keep shaking as they dry. Wash synthetic-pads by hand or machine and tumble dry. Do not dry clean – the filling can absorb toxic cleaning fluid fumes. Wash foam pads gently in warm soapy water. Rinse, squeeze well and dry in a warm place, away from direct heat.

- Press covers while damp to iron out creases.

Glossary

Appliqué
A design created when one fabric or shape is applied to another.

Bias
The diagonal line of fabric formed when the lengthways grain of the fabric is folded to meet the crossways grain of the fabric.

Bodkin
A large, flat needle with a blunt end and large eye, used for threading ribbon, cord or elastic through narrow channels.

Calico
Strong, cheap woven cotton fabric, available unbleached or bleached.

Damask
Fabric woven with a pattern visible on both sides.

Double hem
When fabric is folded twice so that the raw edge is hidden within the hem.

Flat fell seam
A very tough seam where the raw edge is encased within the seam and both lines of stitching appear on the surface.

French seam
A neat, narrow seam which is really two seams, one enclosed within the other. Ideal for use on sheer fabrics.

Gathering
A running or machine stitch that is pulled up to regulate the fullness of a piece of fabric.

Grain
The direction in which the fibres run in a length of fabric.

Interlining
An extra layer of fabric, placed between the main fabric and lining, to add insulation, thickness and weight.

Ladder stitch
An almost invisible stitch used for securing hems or joining two folded edges on the right sides of the fabric.

MDF
Medium-density fibreboard is a man-made board which is very strong and will not break up or splinter when cut. It comes in thicknesses from 1.5cm (⅝in) to 3.5cm (1½in).

Mitre
A corner seam that neatly joins two hems at right angles to each other.

Muslin
Fine cotton fabric that can be used as a backing.

Open seam
Simplest way to join two pieces of fabric together. Fabrics are placed right sides together, machine stitched along a seam line parallel to the fabric raw edge and then pressed open. Used where a lining will cover the seam and hide any raw edges. Also known as a flat seam.

Organdie
Fine translucent cotton muslin, usually stiffened.

Organza
Thin transparent silk or synthetic dress fabric.

Pattern matching
The professional method used to tack two pieces of a patterned fabric together so that the pattern matches across the seam.

Pattern repeat
The depth of one complete design in a length of fabric, which is then repeated along the cloth.

Pin tucks
Narrow stitch fold which provides a decorative feature.

Piping
Piping is a folded strip of fabric, inserted into a seam as an edging. It can be flat or form a covering for piping cord.

Placket
Fabric used to line an opening or slit for fastenings.

Pre-shrinking
Shrinking fabric and trimmings to prevent shrinkage after they have been made up.

PVA glue
A water-based glue that dries clear.

Quilting
The stitches used to decorate and hold two pieces of fabric, with padding between, in position.

Seam allowance
The area between the seam line and the raw edge. The seam allowance needs to be neatened, especially on fabric that frays easily.

Seam line
The line designated for stitching the seam.

Selvage
The non-fraying, tightly-woven edge running down both side edges of a length of fabric.

Tacking
A temporary stitch to hold fabrics in position and act as a guide for permanent stitching.

Tog rating
Duvets are tog rated according to their warmth. The higher the rating the more warmth they will provide. The normal summer rate being 4.5 tog and the winter rate 13.5 tog.

Toile de jouy
A traditional French printed cotton which is perfect for bedrooms. It falls and drapes well, is usually washable and always good to handle.

Topstitch
A line of stitching on the right side of the fabric, often used as a decorative highlight.

Valance
Bed valances fit over the divan base and along one to four sides, depending on the style of the bed.

Wadding
Bonded fabric, in various thicknesses, used to add depth and warmth to another fabric.

Zigzag stitch
Machine stitch used to neaten seams and as a decorative stitch.

Index

Bedrooms and Bathrooms

Credits and acknowledgements.

*The author and publishers would like to thank the following for
their assistance in producing this book:*

For the generous provision of fabric, accessories and props: Osborne and Little, London; F R
Street, Wickford, Essex; Laura Ashley, Newtown, Powys; Offray Ribbons, Co. Tipperary,
Ireland; Titley and Marr, Liss, Hants; Cullingford Carpets, Wincanton, Somerset; Tile Wise
Ltd, Yeovil, Somerset; Charles & Dickens, West Coker, Yeovil, Somerset.

Photographic Credits
Key: t – top, b – bottom, – left, r – right
Elizabeth Whiting & Associates: On 'Contents' page: 'Before You Begin'. All pictures on p6,
tr, bl & *br* on p7, all on pages 8, 9, 10, 11 and tr on p13 / The Design Archives: *tl* on p7 / Dorma-CV
Home Furnishings Ltd: *tl* & *bl* on p13

Written by:	Heather Luke
Managing Editor:	Susan Penny
Art director:	Graham Webb
Designers:	Design Section
Photography:	George Wright
Picture research:	Nell Hunter
Illustrator:	Geoff Denny Associates
Production controller:	Louise McIntyre

Heather Luke has asserted her right to be
identified as the author of this work

First published 1998

© Haynes Publishing 1998

Published by Haynes Publishing
Sparkford, Nr Yeovil, Somerset BA22 7JJ

British Library Cataloguing-in-Publication Data:
A catalogue record of this book is available from
the British Library

ISBN 1 85960 3173

Printed in France by
Imprimerie Pollina S.A., n° 73380-D

While every effort is taken to ensure the accuracy
of the information given in this book, no liability
can be accepted by the author or the publisher for
any loss, damage or injury caused by errors in, or
omissions from the information given.